Y0-ASW-752

WITHDRAWN FROM
M.B.I. LIBRARY

OTHER STUDY NOTES AVAILABLE:

An Uncompromising Life	(Dan. 1, 6, 9:1-19)
The Coming King	(Dan. 7-8)
Christ and the Law	(Mt. 5:17-20)
Living Without Hypocrisy	(Mt. 6:1-8, 16-18)
The Disciples' Prayer	(Mt. 6:9-15)
The Master's Men	(Mt. 10:1-4)
Hallmarks of Discipleship	(Mt. 10:24-42)
Jesus' Teaching on Divorce	(Mt. 19:1-12; Sel.)
The Courage of Commitment	(Jn. 13:31-38; Sel.)
The Comforter Is Coming!	(Jn. 14:15-27)
Jesus' High-Priestly Prayer	(Jn. 17)
Exalting the Crucified Christ	(Ac. 2:14-42)
The Salvation Controversy: Law or Grace?	(Ac. 15:1-16:10)
God: How to Know and Glorify Him	(Ac. 17:22-34; Sel.)
For the Love of the Church	(Ac. 20 & 27)
The Wrath of God	(Rom. 1:16-23)
The Security of Salvation	(Rom. 5:1-11; Sel.)
Giving Up to Gain	(1 Cor. 8-9, 10:23-11:1)
Perfect Love	(1 Cor. 13:1-7)
Resurrection Truth	(1 Cor. 15)
God's Plan for Giving	(1 Cor. 16:1-4; Sel.)
Alive in Christ	(Eph. 1:1-2:10)
The Unity of Believers	(Eph. 2:11-3:13)
Turning on Spiritual Power	(Eph. 3:14-21)
High Position, Lowly Walk	(Eph. 4:1-6)
The Walk of the New Man	(Eph. 4:17-5:17)
Living in the Spirit	(Eph. 5:18-20)
Family Feuding: How to End It	(Eph. 5:21-6:4)
The Believer's Armor	(Eph. 6:10-24)
The Fruitful Life	(Col. 1:1-23)
Living the Risen Life	(Col. 3-4)
The New Covenant	(Heb. 7-10)
The Power of Faith	(Heb. 11:1-12:4)
Christian Ethics	(Heb. 13)
The Church: The Body of Christ	(Selected)
God, Satan, and Angels	(Selected)
The Christ of Christmas	(Selected)
The Second Coming	(Selected)
Is the Bible Reliable?	(Selected)
Triumph over Death	(Selected)
Spiritual Bootcamp	(Selected)
Lighting the Path	(Selected)
True Worship	(Selected)

John MacArthur, Jr.

SPIRITUAL BOOTCAMP
Video/Film Edition

Study Notes

Selected Scripture

Edited and Outlined by David Sper
© 1983 Word of Grace Communications

These study notes are taken from the audio portion of the video/film series **"Spiritual Bootcamp,"** delivered by Pastor-Teacher John MacArthur, Jr. This four-part series is available in video cassette, audio cassette, and in 16mm film. To purchase this series, please consult the current price list; then send your order, making your checks payable to:

WORD OF GRACE COMMUNICATIONS
P.O. Box 4000
Panorama City, CA 91412

Reproduction for Resale Is Prohibited

CONTENTS

I. HOW TO STUDY THE BIBLE 1
    Tape GC 2030—Selected

II. HOW TO PRAY 23
    Tape GC 2031—Selected

III. HOW TO FELLOWSHIP 44
    Tape GC 2032—Selected

IV. HOW TO WITNESS 67
    Tape GC 2033—Selected

Selected Scriptures   Tape GC 2030

HOW TO STUDY THE BIBLE

Introduction

Let's begin by looking at Joshua 1:8. It says this: *"This book of the law [God's Word] shall not depart out of thy mouth, but thou shalt meditate therein day and night, that thou mayest observe to do according to all that is written therein; for then thou shalt make thy way prosperous, and then thou shalt have good success."* Everybody wants success and prosperity, don't they? Well, the Bible says that success and prosperity come right from the pages of Scripture itself. So, let's talk a little bit about how to study God's Word meaningfully. Only then can it bring you the prosperity and success that God promises.

QUESTION #1: *John, with all the volumes of religious material that have been written over man's history, how can we be sure that the Bible is, in fact, the Word of God?*

A. The Bible's Verification

The testimony of the ages is that the Bible can be verified as the Word of God many different ways. For example:

1. EXPERIENCE

    People do what the Bible says, and their lives are changed. Now we don't want to make more out of that than we should, but it is a legitimate way to defend the truth of the Word of God. In other words, if the Bible says, "Christ can give you peace," and you receive Christ and get peace, then that's a verification of its truth, isn't it? Experience, then, verifies the truth of Scripture.

2. SCIENCE

    Scientifically, the Bible is amazingly accurate. For example, the Bible says, *"He . . . hangeth the earth upon nothing"* (Job 26:7). That scientific fact is found in the oldest book in the Bible . . . and there are many others. For example, the hydrological cycle is accurately described in Job 36:27, Psalm 135:7, and Isaiah 55:10.

3. ARCHAEOLOGY

    The Bible gives historical accounts, stories of wars, locations of ancient cities, the existence of lost civilizations, and many other things that were once thought to be historically inaccurate. As archaeologists uncover the ruins of the Middle East, however, the Bible is being verified as accurate.

4. MIRACLES

   The Bible is full of miracles, which is what one would expect in a book about God. The miraculous nature of the Bible speaks of God.

5. PROPHECY

   I think that the greatest proof of the Bible is fulfilled prophecy. God said certain things would happen, and they happened. For example, the destruction of Babylon was predicted in Isaiah 13:19, and the destruction of Tyre was predicted in Ezekiel 26. The odds of all the specific details of just these two prophecies happening by chance are astronomical. Yet, they were all fulfilled. The Bible is verified as the Word of God by the hundreds of prophecies that have already been fulfilled.

B. The Bible's Claims

The testimony of the Bible is just overwhelming. It makes claims for itself that are astounding. For example, the Bible claims to be . . .

1. INFALLIBLE

   In Psalm 19, the Bible says, *"The law of the LORD is perfect . . ."* (v. 7a). In other words, it's infallible, it's without flaw, it's without error.

2. COMPLETE

   In Proverbs 30 it says, *"Add thou not unto His words . . ."* (v. 6a). And in Revelation 22:18-19, the Bible ends with a warning to not take anything away from it or to add anything to it. In other words, the Bible is just the way God wanted it. There's nothing missing—it's total, complete, and thorough.

3. SUFFICIENT

   In 2 Timothy 3, the Apostle Paul told Timothy that the Scriptures were able to make him *"wise unto salvation"* (v. 15b), and that they were able to make the man of God *"perfect, thoroughly furnished unto all good works"* (v. 17b). So, the Bible does a complete job on the human heart and the human soul.

4. AUTHORITATIVE

   Isaiah 1:2 says, *"Hear, O heavens, and give ear, O earth; for the LORD hath spoken . . . ."* When God speaks, everybody ought to listen. That's exactly what Isaiah the prophet was saying.

5. DETERMINATIVE

   In John 8:47, our Lord was talking to some of the Jewish people, and He made the following statement: *"He that is of God heareth God's words; ye, therefore, hear them not, because ye are not of God."* In other words, you can tell a person's destiny by how they relate to the pages of the Word of God.

6. EFFECTIVE

   Isaiah 55:11 says that God's Word will never return void, but will accomplish the purpose that He intends for it to accomplish.

What I say about the Bible is this: If you're going to lay out all the religious books of the world to see which one is true, here's how to handle the Bible. Just open it up and let it speak for itself. Like a lion, you don't defend it; you just open the cage and let it out. It will take care of itself. So, we study the Bible instead of other religious books, because of the claims that it makes, and because of the dynamic way it supports those claims by the things that it does in the lives of the people who commit themselves to it.

QUESTION #2: *Why should we study the Bible?*

A. The Bible Is the Source of Life

We need to study God's Word because it is the source of life. Now the Greeks had two words which we translate *life*. One of the words was *bios*, from which we get our English word *biology*—the study of life. The word *bios* refers to organic life—life as opposed to death. But the Greeks had another word for life (*zōē*), which referred to authentic, meaningful, fulfilling life. The Bible is not the source of biological life—your parents are, with the help of God's creative hand. But the Bible *is* the source of meaningful living. Jesus said, *". . . Man shall not live by bread alone, but by every word that proceedeth out of the mouth of God"* (Mt. 4:4).

So, God's Word provides life and injects it with all that makes life worth living. Have you ever heard someone say, "Life doesn't have any meaning to me. There's no purpose in life. I can't find any value in life"? Do you know why people say that? Because they don't know God's standards and principles. But once they begin to live their lives according to the Word of God, life takes on a full, rich, and exciting meaning.

B. The Bible Is the Source of Truth

I remember walking along Lake Geneva, Wisconsin, one day, when I saw a lady with a T-shirt on that had the following statement: "Personally, I have abandoned my search for the truth."

That's a profound and cynical philosophy, isn't it? In John 18:38, when Pilate said, *"What is truth?,"* I think he had already given up on finding it, too.

We have a lot of information today, don't we? We have computers spitting out information by the ton. I understand there are about three to four thousand new books published in America every day. Now, that's a lot of information! But even with the millions of pages of technological literature and data being constantly pumped out, you begin to get a feeling for what the Apostle Paul said in 2 Timothy 3:7: *"Ever learning, and never able to come to the knowledge of the truth."* Real truth is life-changing truth—transforming truth. It makes a difference in the way you view life, death, time, and eternity. And men are searching for this truth.

In John 17, while our Lord was praying to the Father, He said, *". . . Thy word is truth"* (v. 17b). If you really want truth, it's in the Bible. You can look through the millions of books on the bookshelves of any public or university library . . . but only one of them has the truth, right? And that one book is the Word of God. Do you want to know the truth about God, man, heaven, hell, past, present, and future? Do you want to know the truth about emotions, feelings, and attitudes? It's all in the Bible. That's why we study it.

C. The Bible Is the Source of Power

1. THE POWER OF CONVICTION

Hebrews 4:12 says, *"For the word of God is living, and powerful, and sharper than any two-edged sword, piercing even to the dividing asunder of soul and spirit, and of the joints and marrow, and is a discerner of the thoughts and intents of the heart."* Now, one way in which the Bible shows its power is that it gets inside of us and cuts us up a little bit, doesn't it? Have you ever been reading the Bible, when all of a sudden you come to a verse that convicts you of something that's wrong in your life? You feel like you've just been stabbed, don't you? Well, that's the power of the Word of God as it's expressed in conviction.

It's so important that the Bible convict us of our sin. Let me show you why. Pain is a good thing. Do you know why? Pain tells us that we have a problem. And once we know that we have a problem, we can take care of it, right? If we didn't feel any pain, we could kill ourselves without realizing what was happening. So, pain is a good thing. Well, God has given us another good thing—conviction. Pain tells us that something's wrong with our body, and conviction tells us that something's wrong with our soul. And nothing pierces the soul as much as the truth of the Word of God.

So, when you're studying the Word of God on a daily basis, you're opening up your life, your heart, and your soul to God and saying, "Okay, God, stick me where I need to be stuck, so I know where there's a problem. I want to be all that You want me to be." There is a power, then, in the Word of God in the sense of conviction.

2. THE POWER OF SALVATION

In Romans 1:16, Paul says, *"For I am not ashamed of the gospel of Christ; for it is the power of God unto salvation to everyone that believeth . . . ."* Not only does the Bible convict us of sin, it also has the power to save us from sin and transform our lives. The Word of God has life-changing, soul-changing power. That's why we want to study it.

3. THE POWER OF CHANGED RELATIONSHIPS

In Colossians 3:16-4:1, we find that the Word of God expresses power in our lives in the way that it changes our relationship with God and with others. Verse 16 starts out, *"Let the word of Christ dwell in you richly . . . ."* Now, we know that that expresses power because of what follows. When the Word of Christ dwells in you richly, what happens?

a. **The Generation of Joy and Praise**

The first thing that happens when the Word of Christ dwells in you richly is that you speak to yourselves in *"psalms and hymns and spiritual songs singing with grace in your hearts to the Lord"* (v. 16b). In other words, it has the power to cause you to have a right relationship with God by creating joy and generating praise in your life.

b. **The Ability to Submit to One Another**

Another thing that happens when the Word of Christ dwells in you richly, is that it enables you to submit to one another. God's Word has a way of breaking down pride, so that we can *"look not every man on his own things, but every man also on the things of others"* (Phil. 2:4). According to Colossians 3:18-4:1, husbands and wives, children and parents, and employers and employees are all able to have right relationships with each other when the Word of Christ dwells in them richly.

4. THE POWER OF TRANSFORMATION

In Romans 12:1-2, Paul says, *"I beseech you therefore, brethren, by the mercies of God, that ye present your bodies a living sacrifice, holy, acceptable unto God, which is your reasonable service. And be not conformed to this world, but be ye transformed by the renewing of your mind . . . ."* When the Word of God gets in your mind, it transforms you from the things of this world to the things of God. So, it has the power to separate you from the system. It pulls you away from the love for things of the world, and plants in your heart a love for the things of God.

Let's talk about another thing the Bible does when you study it. The Bible is the source of life, truth, power, and . . .

D. The Bible Is the Source of Happiness

When I use the word *happiness*, I'm not talking about a silly, giddy, childish kind of superficial happiness; I'm referring to true blessedness (to use the biblical term). And by the way, when you see the word *blessed* in the Bible, it means "happy." For example, when the Bible says, *"Blessed is the man,"* it means "Happy is the man." Proverbs 8:34 simply says, *"Blessed [happy] is the man who heareth Me . . . ."* And in Luke 11:28, our Lord says, *". . . blessed are they that hear the word of God, and keep it."*

I really believe that true happiness in life comes out of living according to the Word of God—having the Word of God so saturate your thinking process that it controls your daily living. Let me show you why: We were made for God, right? Colossians 1:16 says that *"all things were created by Him, and for Him."* Now, since we were made for God, we won't really know true happiness until we know a right relationship with Him. And we won't know how to rightly relate to God until we know what His manual says. So, as we study His Word and learn the principles by which we should live, we get in line with God. And once we're at peace with our Maker, God gives us great satisfaction and happiness. Happiness, then, comes as a result of studying the Word of God.

★ The Weeping Prophet that Was Happy

Do you remember the Old Testament prophet by the name of Jeremiah? He's known as the weeping prophet because the people didn't respond to his message. In Jeremiah 1:5, God told Jeremiah, *"Before I formed thee in the womb, I knew thee; and before thou camest forth out of the womb, I sanctified thee, and I ordained thee a prophet unto the nations."* Then God said, "PS, no one will listen to anything you ever say." Now, how's that for a commission? No wonder he was always crying! However, look at Jeremiah 15:16. Jeremiah says, *"Thy words were found, and I did eat them . . . ."* In other words, "Nobody listened but me. I found Your truth, but I was the only one listening." Then he says, *". . . and Thy word was unto me the joy and rejoicing of mine heart . . . ."* Isn't that great? He's saying, "Even if the whole world doesn't listen, I listen. And what I heard was joyful."

I can promise you that when you get into the Word of God and hear what God wants out of your life, and you enter into a right relationship with Him, and you start hearing His promises and all of the things that God's prepared for those that love Him, it can't do anything but produce joy. Maybe you're having problems in a relationship, or maybe your home isn't all that it ought to be, or maybe you don't have the money you need for a certain thing, or maybe you're struggling through school. Maybe all these things aren't the way they ought to be, but I'll tell you one thing: it's all going to work out in the end. Why? Because God's promises in Christ are going to be fulfilled in you. So, the more you study the Bible, the more you will rejoice. Even though the whole world may miss God's promises, they will bring great joy to your heart.

★ The Fellowship of the Burning Heart

In Luke 24:13-32, Jesus was traveling along the road to Emmaus, after His resurrection, when He met two of His disciples who were moaning and groaning because they thought that the Messiah was dead. They never did have much faith, did they? They made up the "little faith" association. Every time He got them into a stressful situation, He had to give them the speech that always started, "O ye of little faith." So, these two disciples believed that it was all over. They had put all their eggs into one basket and the bottom had fallen out. They must have thought, "Here we are, the Messiah's dead, our hope is gone, and the Kingdom didn't materialize." They were moping along on the way to Emmaus, when Jesus joined them. Do you remember what happened? Verse 27 says, *"And beginning at Moses and all the prophets, He expounded unto them, in all the scriptures, the things concerning Himself."* Then they went into a house where He sat down with them and revealed who He was. After He vanished out of their sight, they said to each other, *"Did not our heart burn within us,*

> while He talked with us along the way, and while He opened to us the scriptures?" (v. 32). You see, they were part of the fellowship of the burning heart. The heart is lit on fire with joy, blessedness, and happiness when the truth of Scripture is explained and understood. That's one good reason to study the Word of God.

In Psalm 1:2, the psalmist said, *"But his delight is in the law of the LORD; and in His law doth he meditate day and night."* In Romans 7:22, Paul said, *"For I delight in the law of God . . . ."* And throughout Psalm 119 are verses similar to the following examples: *"Oh, how love I Thy law! It is my meditation all the day"* (v. 97), *". . . Thy law is my delight"* (v. 77b), *"I will delight myself in Thy statutes . . ."* (v. 16a). And it goes on and on. The Bible, then, is the source of life, truth, power, and happiness. Fifth . . .

E. The Bible Is the Source of Growth

1. THE DESIRE FOR GROWTH

   You don't want to stay at the same level of spiritual maturity that you are at right now, do you? You want to develop, become stronger, and have a purer character, right? I think every Christian wants that. When we're children, we want to grow up and be adults. And in the same way, we all want to grow up spiritually. We don't want to be bound by the things we don't know and the things we aren't able to do in the limits of our Christian experience. We want to grow and enjoy the fullness of spiritual life. Well, that only comes through the Word of God.

   In 1 Peter 2:2, Peter says this: *"As newborn babes, desire the pure milk of the word, that ye may grow by it."* What he's doing there is using a very simple analogy. As babies desire milk, that's how you should desire the Bible. How does a baby desire milk? It's a very strong desire, wouldn't you say? Babies really don't desire anything else. Have you ever met a baby who cared what color the curtains were? They don't care. Basically, you just feed a baby and deal with the consequences—that's the beginning and the end of the whole thing. A baby is consumed with the desire for milk. I think that's what Peter is saying. In the same way that a baby has an appetite for one thing, so should you have an appetite for the Word of God. And just as the baby grows because of that milk, you will grow by the Word of God. It's the source of growth, nurturing, and building us up.

2. THE DEGREES OF GROWTH

First John 2:13 is a very important verse in explaining the levels, or degrees, of spiritual growth: *"I write unto you, fathers, because ye have known Him that is from the beginning. I write unto you, young men, because ye have overcome the wicked one. I write unto you, little children, because ye have known the Father."* There are three levels of spiritual growth: little children, young men, and fathers.

a. **Little Children**

When you become a Christian, you are a little child. Literally, the word in verse 13 is *baby*. According to Ephesians 4:14, a spiritual baby is undiscerning. And that's true with a physical baby as well, isn't it? A baby crawls along the floor and sticks anything it finds in its mouth. They're not discerning, are they? They don't know what's good for them and what is not. Little children are the same way. When my children were small, if we had let them eat what they wanted to eat, they would have eaten nothing but ice cream, candy, and cookies. (We still have a problem with that, come to think of it.) When they are little, that's what they'll do. Why? Because they're undiscerning. They don't know what's good for them. The same thing is true about a spiritual baby. Basically, a baby knows that God is their Father, they know their spiritual ABCs, and they can say da-da. But that's about it.

b. **Young Men**

In 1 John 2:14 John writes, *". . . I have written unto you, young men, because ye are strong, and the word of God abideth in you, and ye have overcome the wicked one."* You come to the second level of spiritual growth when the Word of God abides in you. In other words, when you put the principles of the Word of God into practice in your life, you begin to grow, don't you? You leave spiritual babyhood, and are no longer *"tossed to and fro, and carried about with every wind of doctrine"* (Eph. 4:14). Babies are easily victimized by false teaching because they don't know the Word. But when you study the Word and become a spiritual young man, you are able to overcome the wicked one—Satan.

You say, "Can we actually overcome Satan?" Yes, we can! Satan is primarily disguised as an angel of light, so he comes in false religion and false doctrine. But as we know the Word, we're no longer threatened by that. For example, I'm not threatened when I hear about a false doctrine or I read about a false cult. It just makes me mad! I get indignant and want to proclaim the truth. So, when we reach the state where we know the Word, we become spiritual young men. There's a virility, an energy, and a strength that causes us to desire to go out and defend the faith. Satan's false systems don't entice us anymore, they just aggravate us. Spiritual young men want to go out and conquer the world.

Now, there's a third level of spiritual growth:

  c. **Fathers**

At the beginning of 1 John 2:14, John writes, *"I have written unto you, fathers, because ye have known Him that is from the beginning. . . ."* Who do spiritual fathers know? God. Spiritual fathers have reached a certain level of spiritual growth where they know God in a very personal way. It's one thing to know the Book, but it's something else to have an intimate relationship with the God who's behind it. That's where we're headed in our spiritual growth. We're going from the stage of knowing that God saved us (spiritual babyhood), to knowing the Word of God (spiritual young men). The longer you study the Word of God, and the more deeply it finds root in your life, the more you'll begin to see the God who leaks out between the pages, in between the words. Then you'll begin to commune and walk with Him. You've met saints like that, haven't you? Those saints whose lives just oozed a sense of the reality of God—as they walked and talked with the Lord.

Now, that's what it means to grow spiritually. We're all in that process, and the key is the Word of God. We need to desire it with the same kind of desire that a baby has for milk, so that we can grow in that manner.

F. The Bible Is the Source of Ministry

As Christians, we want to reach out to others, right? In 2 Timothy 2:2, Paul said to Timothy, *"And the things that thou hast heard from me among many witnesses, the same commit thou to faithful men, who shall be able to teach others also."* In other words, it's as if you're in a relay race. Somebody gave you the baton, which you're to give to somebody else, so they can pass it on. What is the baton that we were handed? Paul identifies the baton as *"the things that thou hast heard from me."* What were those things? Divine truth. Paul gave Timothy divine truth, and then said, "Timothy, give it to somebody else, so they can give it to somebody else." In other words, it's only as we know the Word of God that we can pass it on to somebody else, who can, in turn, pass it on and keep the relay going.

★ Finishing the Work of Christ

I'm a terrible artist. I found that out when I took some art classes that were required in school. I remember a tiger I drew that everyone laughed at. From then on I only drew stick figures. I had a horrible experience with art because I'm not very good at it. Now what would happen if I were alive during the time of Rembrandt, and he came up to me and said, "Look, MacArthur, I've got to go on a trip, but I haven't finished this portrait. The eyes still need to be done. So would you mind doing them for me?"? Or what if Michelangelo came up to me and said, "I've got to leave town. I'm not quite finished with an angel I'm painting. Would you finish painting the face for me?"? Well, all he would get out of me would be two dots and a smile. I would never lay my hand to a Rembrandt or a Michelangelo!

I was startled, one time, to read what Luke wrote in Acts 1:1: *"The former treatise* [the Gospel of Luke] *have I made, O Theophilus, of all that Jesus began . . . ."* I suddenly realized that the book of Acts is about people finishing what Jesus began—picking up where He left off. All of us in the body of Christ are in that same category. We are finishing the work of Christ. That's a tremendous thought, isn't it? Now, if we're going to be finishing the unfinished work of Christ, we need to be sure we know how to do it, don't we? Where do we find that kind of information? Where do we find out how to love people? Where do we find out how to teach people? Where do we find out what's important in terms of conveying right attitudes and right actions? It's all in God's Word! The Bible is the source of all that information. That's why we study it.

QUESTION #3: *When is the best or most productive time in the day to study the Bible?*

I remember going to a conference, one time, and this guy got up for one hour and said, "You must pray and study the Bible in the morning." "Early will I seek Thee," was his text. Well, as he was banging away trying to prove the point that we are to seek God in the morning, I decided to look up all the places where people prayed and sought God in the afternoon. After I found numerous passages where people sought God in the afternoon, I also found many places where they sought Him in the evening. Then I read Psalm 55:17, which said, *"Evening, and morning, and at noon, will I pray . . . ."* So, I concluded that we're supposed to seek the Lord all the time. In fact, 1 Thessalonians 5:17 says, *"Pray without ceasing,"* and 2 Timothy 2:15 says, *"Study to show thyself approved unto God, a workman that needeth not to be ashamed, rightly dividing the word of truth."* Notice that it doesn't tell us when we're to study, it just tells us to get at it until we're a workman that doesn't need to be ashamed.

I think that studying the Bible is to be a way of life. I've always felt that Christians are to make sure that they are learning something new and fresh—something that they've never seen before—every single day. Look at it this way: Job said that God's Word was more precious to him than his necessary food (Job 23:12). That's an incredible statement! We really don't like to miss a meal, do we? If we go half an hour past our regular lunchtime, some of us start to have real problems. We have to have our food, don't we? But are you that way when it comes to studying the Word of God? You should be! That's very important.

So, to specifically answer the question regarding the best time to study the Bible, I believe we're to study it all the time. And the key to it is what David said in Psalm 119:11: *"Thy word have I hidden in mine heart . . . ."* And in Psalm 1:2, he said to meditate on it day and night. Now there is something to be said for a morning emphasis, because then you'll have something to chew on during the day. But that doesn't mean you're to ignore it the rest of the time. Studying the Word of God is to be a way of life. And remember, the more of God's Word you put in, the more it's going to affect what comes out.

I was recently studying Proverbs 4:20-27, and it essentially says this: "Take in the Word of God with your ears and your eyes, let it settle in your heart, meditate on it, and it will come out like a fountain of spring water in the things that you do and say." That's really true, isn't it? So, first you have to put the Word of God in, then it will begin to flow out of your life.

QUESTION #4: *Who can study the Bible? Do you have to be specially trained to understand it?*

People always say, "I have read the Bible and I don't understand it." Maybe you've said that. Well, let's look at who can study the Bible. To study the Bible with understanding . . .

A. You Must Be a Christian

First Corinthians 2:14 says, *"But the natural man receiveth* [or 'understandeth'] *not the things of the Spirit of God; for they are foolishness unto him, neither can he know them, because they are spiritually discerned."* And since men are spiritually dead, as it says in Ephesians 2:1, they can't understand spiritual truth.

You say, "What does it mean to be spiritually dead?" Well, life is basically the ability to respond to your environment, right? A dead person is unable to respond to his environment. So, a spiritually dead person is unable to respond to the spiritual environment where God lives, speaks, moves, and acts. Without Christ, men are dead to that environment. Now, an unbeliever can read the Bible and understand some of the facts and a little bit of the history, but the whole intent of the message is never going to penetrate his deadness. It isn't until a person becomes alive in Christ that he can understand the Bible. So, to study the Bible effectively, you must, first of all, be a Christian.

★ *Reading in the Dark*

It doesn't do any good for critics to attack the Bible who don't know the living Christ of the Bible. Why? Because they're never going to come up with the right answer anyway. They pass themselves off, very often, as great critics of biblical literature. But the truth of the matter is that they miss the whole point of the passage!

I remember speaking to a philosophy class at a local university. The professor was not a believer, but he liked to have Christians speak to his class every once in awhile so the students could attack the Christian. He asked me to speak on biblical sex ethics, and since I thought it would be fun, I went. Well, speaking on that particular topic on a university campus is a good way to get thrown out fast. So, at the very beginning, I said, "Now, none of you are going to listen to what I say. None of you are going to accept it, or believe it, or care about it. I just want to establish that at the beginning." That's a good way to get the attention of college kids, because they immediately said, "Oh yeah?," and I had them where I wanted them. Then I said, "And the reason you won't be able to accept the things that I'm going to say is this: You don't know the Christ of the Word of God and you don't know and love the God who gave us these truths. And without that relationship, these things are meaningless to you." That's the bottom line.

To understand the truths of the Word of God you must begin by becoming a believer. First Corinthians 2 says, *"But he that is spiritual judgeth all things . . . . [because] we have the mind of Christ"* (vv. 15a, 16b). Isn't that great? When we open the Bible, we can understand it because we have the mind of Christ.

Second, for you to be able to study and understand the Bible, I believe that . . .

B. You Must Be Dealing with Sin

As we saw earlier, 1 Peter 2:2 says, *"As newborn babes, desire the pure milk of the word, that ye may grow by it."* But verse 1 says this: *"Wherefore, laying aside all malice, and all guile: and hypocrisies, and envies, and all evil speakings."* That's where it starts. Then you're to *"desire the pure milk of the word."* If you don't get rid of the garbage in your life, you're not going to have a clean filter to get the truth through. So, in order to study the Bible you must be a Christian, and you must also be dealing with the sin in your life. You must be a pure vessel.

When I begin to study the Bible, I have a little routine that I go through. I just say, "Lord, I want you to purge any sin out of my life and cleanse me." And do you know what that does? It forces me to get my life right if I really want to get anything out of my Bible study. That's very important.

Dealing with sin in your life means that you're confessing your sin. You don't have to be perfect to study the Bible. You don't have to fall out of heaven with a little halo on your head to be able to study the Bible. And you don't have to be sanctimonious, with a special aura about you to be able to understand the Bible. I think that all of us can study the Bible with understanding . . . if we're dealing with the sin in our lives.

A third thing that is very important, if you are going to study the Bible effectively, is that . . .

C. You Must Be Spirit Controlled

Who wrote the Bible? God the Holy Spirit was basically the Author, wasn't He? So, in order to understand the Bible, we have to get in tune with the Author. In 1 John 2 it says that we have an anointing, an unction, from God so that we do not need men to teach us (vv. 20, 27). Do you know what that anointing, that unction, is? It's the Holy Spirit. Do you remember what Jesus promised His disciples when He told them that He was going to go away? He promised to send them *"another Comforter"* (Jn. 14:16). And He also said, *". . . when He, the Spirit of truth, is come, He will guide you into all truth . . . and He will show you things to come"* (Jn. 16:13). The Spirit of God, then, is our Teacher. So, another thing that I always do before I study the Bible is to ask God to fill me with His Spirit.

There was a great preacher, years ago, in England. And it was said that he was the most powerful preacher of his time. He had a habit of spending time in his study, down on his knees, pouring out his heart to God. There were even places worn in the floor where he had knelt and prayed for many years. When it was time for him to preach, he would leave his place of prayer, and walk silently to the pulpit behind a little man called a sexton. And as he climbed up the steps of the pulpit, at each step he would say to himself, "I believe in the Holy Spirit, I believe in the Holy Spirit, I believe in the Holy Spirit," all the way up. Why? Because he knew that the understanding of the Word of God, and the power of its proclamation, was bound up in the Spirit of God.

Let me give you one more point. To study the Bible effectively, you must be saved, you must be dealing with sin in your life, you must be controlled by the Spirit, and . . .

D. You Must Be Prayerful

In Ephesians 1:17-18, Paul prays the following prayer: *"That the God of our Lord Jesus Christ, the Father of glory, may give unto you the spirit of wisdom and revelation in the knowledge of Him, the eyes of your understanding being enlightened; that ye may know . . . ."* And then he goes on to pray about what he wants the Ephesians to know. In other words, Paul says, "I'm praying for you that you'll understand what God has given you."

I think prayer is an important part of Bible study. You never want to go to the Bible thinking, "I'm intelligent enough to handle this. I've got all this stuff figured out." Instead, you need to go to the Bible with the understanding that only by the power of God can you open its spiritual truths. When you depend on Him, you're going to get the answers.

So, who can study the Bible effectively? Someone who is saved, dealing with sin, controlled by the Spirit, and prayerful. In other words, it's available to all of us if we follow certain guidelines. Now, I must also mention that God has given certain men to the church—teachers who are specially gifted by the Spirit—to help the rest of the body to understand His Word better.

QUESTION #5: *How should we study the Bible, John? It's such a big book, and there's so much for us to learn.*

When I first started studying the Bible, I didn't think it was possible for anyone to know the Bible. But at the same time, I had a tremendous desire to know all I could. In fact, to be honest with you, the reason I got into the pastorate was not so much to preach as it was to have the time to study it for myself. I had such a hunger to know God's Word . . . and still do. I was always under the impression, however, that no one could ever get it all. But the longer I study the Bible, the more I'm learning that basically there are sets of principles that just keep getting repeated over and over and over again.

When I was in seminary, I was stunned by what the Apostle Paul said in Acts 20:27. He had only been in Ephesus for three years (Ac. 20:31), yet he was able to say, at the end of that time, *"For I did not shrink from declaring to you the whole counsel of God"* (RSV).

I used to wonder how he could have done that in just three years, but when I got into the story a little bit, I found out that he taught every day from one to five in the afternoon (they didn't work those hours because it was so hot), and then went from house to house and taught them at night. And at the end of three years he was able to say, "I have not failed to declare unto you the whole counsel of God." So I thought to myself, "It can't be that difficult. There has to be a way that God will allow us to know His Word." Let me suggest to you how to get the most out of studying the Bible:

A. Read It

That sounds basic, I know, but most people don't even read their Bibles. To get the most out of Bible study, you must first be committed to reading it. And I'll tell you how to read it: Read it repetitiously. Isaiah 28:10 says, *"For precept must be upon precept, precept upon precept; line upon line, line upon line . . . ."* Now, this verse is in a little different context, but the idea is the same. We learn by repetition.

When I was in college, I decided to read the Bible repetitiously. I started with 1 John and read it straight through. The five chapters took me about twenty-five minutes to read. The next day, I read the entire book straight through again. Now, most people read a verse here, and a verse there—and it's all disjointed. But the books of the Bible have flow, logic, reason, and theme. So, I read 1 John straight through, and I kept reading it every day for thirty days. Well, do you know what happened at the end of thirty days? I knew what was in 1 John. If you were to ask me, "Where does the Bible talk about confessing our sins?" That's easy! First John 1:9, left-hand page, right-hand column, halfway down. When you read repetitiously, you begin to visualize the pages of your Bible and remember where certain passages are located. That's why I always have to use the same Bible. I'm lost without it.

After I finished 1 John, I went to the Gospel of John. Since it has twenty-one chapters, I split it into three sections of seven chapters each, and read each section for thirty days. In ninety days I had finished the Gospel of John. And even to this day, over twenty years later, I can tell you what's in every chapter. This is because while I was reading it, I was making little cards with the theme of each chapter on it, and reviewing them each day. I began to see the Bible come alive and explain itself to me, without even reading any other books.

When I finished 1 John and the Gospel of John, I went to the book of Philippians, then to Matthew—continuing to bounce back and forth from a short book to a long one. Now, if you read the New Testament that way, you'll get through it thirty times every two and one-half years. In the Old Testament, I just read the narrative, and flow through it once or twice each year. But the New Testament is to be read repetitiously.

The second thing you're to do if you're going to get the most out of your Bible study is to . . .

B. Interpret It

Once you find out what the Bible says, you have to find out what it means by what it says. You say, "How do I do that?" Well, this will occur through the following steps:

1. RELATE SCRIPTURE TO OTHER SCRIPTURE

    If you just keep reading the Bible repetitiously, you will find that oftentimes it will interpret itself. For example, let's say you read something about being humble and meek, and you begin to wonder what that means. If you've already spent thirty days in Philippians, verses 3-8 of chapter 2 would probably come to mind immediately. You begin to interpret the Bible by the Bible. So, the key to knowing what it means is basically to know what it says so well that the Spirit of God can interpret it to your own heart. That's a tremendously exciting process. But you need to go a step further.

    In Nehemiah 8, all the people got together, opened the book of the law, and revival came. Do you know why? In verse 8 it says that they not only read the book of the law, but they *"gave the sense, and caused them to understand the reading."* Interpretation begins with reading, but then it must be explained so that it can be understood. That's what a teacher or serious Bible student does, isn't it? It isn't enough to just read the Bible, and say, "Amen! Isn't that wonderful?" And then hope that by osmosis it's going to affect your life, without having any understanding of the passage. You have to go beyond the initial stage of reading it, and begin to . . .

2. USE STUDY TOOLS

    Now this means that maybe it would be good for you to get a Bible dictionary, a good Bible commentary, a concordance, and any other pertinent resource material. Christian bookstores are loaded with Bible study tools, and you need to take advantage of what is available. So, after you've done your reading for the day, you need to set aside some time to take a passage—whatever passage you choose, in whatever book you choose—and just work through it a little bit each day, using the various study tools. Also . . .

3. ASK YOURSELF QUESTIONS

   The key way to interpret a passage is to ask yourself questions. When I get ready to teach, or preach a sermon, or exegete a passage, or write a book, I read the passage, and then I ask questions like, "What does this mean? Why is that phrase used there? What does the writer mean by this?" and so on.

4. PURSUE THE ANSWERS

   Once I write all the questions down, I know what I need to know. Then I pursue the answers to all my questions. That's how the unfolding of the text takes place.

   Now, one thing I need to warn you of: As you interpret the Bible, it's very important to . . .

5. ESTABLISH THE CONTEXT

   The key to all Bible interpretation is the context. You don't ever want to take a verse out of context. Like the guy who taught that it was a sin for girls to have their hair up on top of their head because the Bible says, ". . . *top not come down* . . . ." Well, Matthew 24:17 does say that! However, the entire verse says, *"Let him who is on the housetop not come down to take anything out of his house."* If you take verses and rip them out of their context, you can make the Bible say whatever you want. Like the guy who put the following verses together: ". . . [Judas] *went and hanged himself.* . . . *Go, and do thou likewise.* . . . *What thou doest, do quickly"* (Mt. 27:5b; Lk. 10:37b; Jn. 13:27b). Well, that's all in the Bible, but somebody put it together wrong! Context is everything.

   Now, to establish the context of a passage, you have to ask yourself, "What's going on before this? What's going on after this? What's the historical setting?" and so forth. You see, when you study the Bible, you have to close certain gaps. One gap you have to close is the language gap, right? The Bible was written in Greek, Hebrew, and some Aramaic, so you have to have some help there. Frankly, we're fortunate to have the Bible in English. That gives us a good start. But there is also a culture gap, a geography gap, and a history gap. So, as you begin to close those gaps, you begin to establish the context.

Now, after you read the Bible and interpret it, you must also . . .

C. **Meditate on It**

It's important that you meditate on the Word of God. I find that after I've done all my study, the best thing for me to do is to sit back and think through that passage . . . over and over again.

Then, at the end of my meditating process, I like to talk it through with somebody else. It really helps to be able to sit down with somebody else and say, "Hey, I have some ideas about the meaning of this passage, what do you think? What are your thoughts on this verse?" and so on. And as you dialogue, you begin to gain even more insight into what you are studying. Proverbs 27:17 says, *"Iron sharpeneth iron; so a man sharpeneth the countenance of his friend."* So, as you interact with one another, it becomes very helpful.

After you've read the Bible, interpreted it, and meditated on it, if you really want to understand it, the final step is to . . .

D. Teach It

In order to teach the Bible to somebody else, you have to know it yourself. It's very easy to be hard to understand. I could confuse you very easily. All I have to do is not know what I'm talking about. But do you know how hard it is to be clear and easily understood? You have to thoroughly understand your subject before you can teach clearly. So, once you have the responsibility to teach somebody else, you're really going to know what you believe. And that's when you're going to know the Word of God.

Well, the Bible's a great book, isn't it? It promises that if you study it, your way will be prosperous and you'll have good success (Josh. 1:8). Of all the books in the world, it's the only book to really study, because it's the authoritative Word of the living God. We ought to study it because it is the source of all that we really need and want. And as we study it and meditate on it, we then have the responsibility to know how to interpret it rightly, so that we can fully understand its truths.

Now, having said all that, let me say this: Even if we followed all these steps, we still wouldn't be able to understand the Bible if God hadn't been gracious enough to give us the Holy Spirit to be our Teacher. And that's a wonderful thing to remember, so we don't get too proud or independent. It also gives us a wonderful confidence, because we know our own inabilities. God bless you as you study His Word.

Focusing on the Facts

1. What are the five ways that the Bible can be verified as the Word of God? (see pp. 1-2)
2. What are the six claims that the Bible makes for itself? (see pp. 2-3)
3. We should study the Bible because it is the source of what six important elements? (see pp. 3-10)
4. Why should we study the Bible, according to Matthew 4:4? (see p. 3)

5. What is the key to a full, rich, and meaningful life? (see p. 3)

6. What is the only source of real, life-changing truth? Give a scriptural reference to verify your answer. (see p. 4)

7. What are the four ways that the Bible shows us its power? (see pp. 4-6)

8. Hebrews 4:12 describes the power of the Word of God as it's expressed in _____. Why is this characteristic of Scripture so important to our daily walk with God? (see pp. 4-5)

9. According to Colossians 3:16-4:1, what happens when the Word of Christ dwells in us richly? (see p. 5)

10. Practically speaking, how does the Word of God transform our lives? (see p. 6)

11. Why does happiness come as a result of studying the Bible? (see p. 6)

12. Who was known as the weeping prophet? Why? What was it that brought joy and rejoicing to his heart? (see pp. 6-7)

13. How did the psalmist view the law of the Lord? (see p. 8)

14. What is the source of spiritual growth in the life of every Christian? What is the point of Peter's analogy in 1 Peter 2:2? (see p. 8)

15. What are the three levels of spiritual growth according to 1 John 2:13? How are each of these levels described? (see pp. 9-10)

16. What analogy does Paul use in 2 Timothy 2:2? What is the truth he is trying to convey? (see pp. 10-11)

17. When is the best time of the day to study the Bible? Explain your answer. (see pp. 11-12)

18. What are the effects of meditating on Scripture throughout the day? (see p. 12)

19. What are the four prerequisites to effective Bible study? (see pp. 12-15)

20. What does it mean to be spiritually dead? Why can't someone who is spiritually dead understand the Bible? (see p. 13)

21. According to 1 Peter 2:1-2, what must we do before we attempt to study God's Word? Why? (see p. 14)

22. What is the *"unction"* and the *"anointing"* referred to by John in 1 John 2:20 and 27? How does this relate to the effectiveness of our Bible study? (see p. 14)

23. Why is it important to be prayerful when you study the Bible? (see p. 15)

24. How long did it take the Apostle Paul to teach *"the whole counsel of God"* to the Ephesians? How was he able to do this? (see pp. 15-16)
25. What are the four general steps which make up the proper method of Bible study? (see pp. 16-19)
26. What's the best way to read the New Testament? Why? What's the best way to read the Old Testament? (see pp. 16-17)
27. What are the steps for proper biblical interpretation? (see pp. 17-18)
28. After you have interpreted a passage, what should you do to gain more insight into its meaning? (see p. 18)
29. The best way to really understand the Bible is to teach it. Why is this true? (see p. 19)

Pondering the Principles

1. The Bible can be verified as the Word of God by experience, science, archaeology, miracles, and prophecy. When someone challenges your belief that the Bible is the Word of God, which of these verifications do you rely on the most? Why? Which of these verifications do you think is the most effective in convincing a skeptic that the Bible is the Word of God? Why?
2. The Bible claims to be infallible, complete, sufficient, authoritative, determinative, and effective. Define each of these claims and discuss why each one is so important in your life.
3. We should study the Bible because it is the source of life, truth, power, happiness, growth, and ministry. Considering each of these reasons for Bible study separately, what consequences will occur in the life of a Christian who does not study the Bible? Be specific!
4. People are always looking for answers to their problems. And we know that the only source of truth is the Bible. What are some of the issues that people are facing today? What questions are they seeking answers to? Make a list of these questions, then try and answer each one from the Word of God. Remember: First Peter 3:15 says, *". . . be ready always to give an answer to every man that asketh you . . . ."*
5. How does the Bible express its power in the life of an unbeliever? How does it express its power in the life of a believer? When was the last time you experienced one of the facets of its power, and what occurred specifically? Since you've become a Christian, in what ways have you become separated from the world and transformed in your thinking?

6. How often should you study the Bible? How often *do* you study the Bible? Do you find that studying the Bible is most productive at a particular time of day? If so, when is it, and why is that the best time for you? Why is it essential to be in the Word on a daily basis? What new truths have you learned this week?

7. There are some prerequisites to be able to read and study the Bible with understanding. You must be: a Christian, dealing with sin, Spirit controlled, and prayerful. If you are having problems understanding the Bible, which of these prerequisites aren't you fulfilling? What's a good habit to get into before you attempt to study God's Word?

8. Is there a particular method of Bible reading that you have found helpful? If so, what is it? What is your reaction to the repetitive reading plan of one book a day for thirty days? Discuss the benefits and the possible pitfalls of this particular reading plan.

9. What should come first: interpreting a passage or meditating upon it? Why? What's the best way to interpret a passage? What role does meditation play in the overall understanding of Scripture? Why will the responsibility of teaching encourage your spiritual growth?

Selected Scriptures   Tape GC 2031

HOW TO PRAY

Introduction

In this lesson, we're going to be looking at a great subject—the subject of prayer. And I think a good way to start would be to look at a couple of verses in Romans 8. In verse 16 Paul says, *"The Spirit Himself beareth witness with our spirit, that we are the children of God."* There's a sense in which the Holy Spirit confirms in our hearts that we belong to God. Backing up to verse 15, Paul gives us a little better insight into the extent of this confirmation: *"For ye have not received the spirit of bondage again to fear; but ye have received the Spirit of adoption, whereby we cry, Abba, Father."* This was an incredible thought to a Jewish person who was raised with the understanding that God was far off and unapproachable, behind a veil somewhere. When the Jews were at the foot of Mount Sinai, there was thunder and smoke and lightning . . . and a tremendous amount of fear. Hebrews 12:29 says, *"For our God is a consuming fire."* So, for somebody to say that we can cry, *"Abba, Father,"* was an unbelievable thought, because *"Abba"* means "pappa" or "daddy."

How is it that a person can come to God—the great God of the universe—with that kind of intimacy, and with that kind of access? Well, that's really what prayer is all about. I want to talk about the essence of what it means to come into the presence of an infinitely holy, awesome, majestic God, with the feeling that we are not only welcome, but that He longs to have us there. Prayer is an essential part of our Christian experience, so I hope I can answer the questions that are on your heart concerning this tremendous subject.

QUESTION #1: *If God knows our hearts, and He knows all things, why are we to pray?*

A lot of people ask that question. In other words, "If God is in control, and God is sovereign, why should we bother to pray? Isn't He going to do whatever He wants anyway?" Well, there is a basic problem with that kind of reasoning. Essentially, you're saying, "If I can't figure God out on my terms, then I won't respond to Him . . . no matter what He says!" There *are* reasons to pray—five of them. The first reason that we are to pray is . . .

A. It Is Commanded

We are to pray because we're commanded to pray. In Ephesians 6:18, it says that we are to be *"praying always with all prayer and supplication."* Now the context of that command is important. Paul talks about the armor of God that we are to have on if we're to be victorious in our battle against Satan and his demons (6:11-17). Then, in verse 18, he gives us a command to pray.

Now, if you say, "Well, I know it's commanded, but I don't know how important it is," what you're really saying is, "If I can't figure out how my prayers fit into God's plan, then I'm not going to respond to His command." You don't want to do that. Our responsibility is to obey God.

★ Accepting the Paradoxes of Scripture

The Bible contains many paradoxes—things that we can't resolve in our own minds. Let me give you a few illustrations:

1. WHO WROTE THE BIBLE? For example, who wrote Ephesians? "Paul wrote Ephesians," you say. Well, did he just sit down one day and write Ephesians . . . all by himself? No, God inspired him, didn't He? Now, if God wrote Ephesians, and Paul wrote Ephesians, who wrote what part? "Well," you say, "they both wrote it!" But how do you explain that it was all of Paul and all of God? You can't resolve it, can you? That is what's called an apparent paradox. You can't harmonize it. Now, if you try to harmonize it, you're going to either eliminate Paul's personality or God's inspiration. You just have to let the tension stay there.

2. IS JESUS GOD OR MAN? Someone might say, "He's a man." But somebody else might say, "He's God." What's the answer? He's both. And if you try to resolve that, your only options are that He is half God and half man, all man and no God, or all God and no man. None of those options are acceptable, so we have to learn to live with the tension. Now, whenever you take the divine world and try to reduce it to a level of human understanding, you're going to have problems. Why? Because of the limitation of the human mind. We have to realize that from the very beginning.

3. WHO LIVES YOUR CHRISTIAN LIFE? You say, "I do! I beat my body to bring it into subjection, I discipline myself, and I say no to sin and yes to God." That's good, but in Galatians 2:20 Paul said, ". . . *nevertheless I live; yet not I, but Christ liveth in me* . . . ." So, who

lives your Christian life, you or Christ? You say, "He does what's good and I do what's bad." Well, that's not true. Some of the good that we do is initiated by our own will, isn't it? And yet, He is to receive all the glory.

4. HOW DID YOU BECOME A CHRISTIAN? When you were saved, did you come to Jesus Christ because you were chosen by God before the foundation of the world? Yes. But did you come because your heart responded? Yes. You see, we have to learn to live with the tensions of Scripture.

When we pray, we have to learn to accept the tension that is there. We have to be able to say, "I'm going to pray because I'm commanded to pray. Even though God is in control of the universe, I will obey Him, and not imagine that I, as a human being, need to resolve all the mysteries of the divine mind." So, the first reason we are to pray is that we are commanded to pray. A second reason to pray is . . .

B. It Is a Sin Not to Pray

In 1 Samuel 12:23, Samuel said, ". . . *God forbid that I should sin against the* LORD *in ceasing to pray for you . . . ."* In this verse, Samuel is talking to the people of Israel, and referring to the responsibility he had to pray for them. God expects us to bring one another before Him in prayer. In fact, in James 5:16 we're commanded to *"pray one for another."* So, it's a sin not to pray.

A third reason we are to pray is . . .

C. It Gives Glory to God

I believe that we are to pray because it gives glory to God. In John 14, during the Last Supper, Jesus was sharing His heart with His disciples and giving them insights into what they needed to know in His absence. One of the marvelous things He told them is recorded for us in verse 13. He said, *"And whatever ye shall ask in My name, that will I do . . . ."* Now, that's a tremendous promise, isn't it? Then He added, *". . . that the Father may be glorified . . . ."* You see, that's the reason God answers prayer—so that He will be glorified. In other words, prayer isn't primarily to give us what we want. Now, I do think that God cares that we have clothes, food, a place to stay, and other things. In fact, God has poured out many blessings that we are the recipients of. And I do think that God blesses us through prayer. But the primary reason for prayer is to put God on display.

For example, when you pray for a friend, or somebody you know, to be saved, and they come to Christ, what's your first response? Do you think to yourself, "Wow, am I ever a powerful pray-er!"? Is that your response? No. What is your response? "Thank You, Lord." Why? Because you know that salvation comes from God. God, then, is put on display. Now let's say that you weren't praying for that person when they came to Christ. God still saved the person, but you did not see the glory of God manifested through your prayers, because you weren't involved. Have you ever gone to a prayer meeting where somebody has gotten up and said, "So-and-so has come to Christ," or "So-and-so has been delivered from an illness," or "So-and-so got a job," or "So-and-so had a relationship restored," and they were excited . . . but you were sitting there yawning and indifferent to the whole thing? Well, you were indifferent because you were not involved in the prayer process. And if you're not involved in the prayer process, then you're not going to be involved in the rejoicing. You're not going to be able to say, "Praise God! What a tremendous thing He has done." God wants us to be *"praying always"* (Eph. 6:18a), so that we're always seeing Him display His power firsthand. That's when we're really able to give Him glory.

As you look, then, at the matter of prayer, realize that it's not utilitarian. Don't back off and ask some theological question like, "Well, if You're going to do what You're going to do anyway, why should I get involved?" That's the wrong question to ask. Rather, your question should be, "How can I get involved in praying for as much as I possibly can, so that I can see God put His glory on display?" You see, when God answers prayer, He's displaying divine power in action, as well as divine mercy, divine grace, divine love, and all of His other attributes.

Now, that leads me to a fourth principle. We should pray because . . .

D. It Lines Us Up with God's Purposes

When we pray, we shouldn't be trying to line God up with our purposes, we should be trying to get our hearts lined up with His. I always think of the little kid who was kneeling beside his bed one night, praying, "God bless Mommy, and God bless Daddy," and then at the top of his voice, "and God, I want a new bicycle!" His mom stopped him and said, "Hey, God isn't deaf, you know." He replied, "Yeah, I know. But Grandma's in the next room and she's hard of hearing." He wasn't interested in what God wanted, was he? He was only interested in what *he* wanted—believing that if God couldn't handle it, Grandma could.

We don't like to admit it, but a lot of our prayers are like that. Oftentimes, we pray with the idea that we're going to get God lined up with our purposes. We pray, "Lord, if You'll just do this, or give me that, I'll do thus-and-so." But the whole purpose of prayer is to line us up with God's purposes. As we commune with Him in prayer, we begin to feel His heart and line ourselves up with Him.

For example, in Matthew 6, when Jesus taught His disciples how to pray, notice how the prayer started: *"Our Father, who art in heaven, Hallowed be Thy name. Thy kingdom come. Thy will be done in earth, as it is in heaven"* (vv. 9-10). He never got to the "us" part of the prayer—*"Give us this day our daily bread. And forgive us our debts . . ."* (vv. 11-12)—until He had gotten through the part that pertained to God's purposes. In other words, Jesus was saying, "When you pray, before you get to your own needs, start by lining up your heart with God's eternal purposes."

Prayer is the vehicle that allows us to get in harmony, in symphony, with the divine purpose of God. That's a tremendous concept we need to understand. And once we understand it, we're not going to pray as if God were some utilitarian genie that comes out of a little bottle, to whom we can say, "All right, God. I get three wishes . . . fast! You've promised me that in Christ I can have whatever I want. Now You're stuck . . . so deliver!" Prayer is to line up your own heart with God's purposes. That makes prayer very unselfish, doesn't it?

A fifth reason to pray is that . . .

E. It Results in Answers

I believe that God answers prayer. Is that a simple enough reason to pray? Don't start asking me about how the theology of that works out, because I don't know! People say, "How can someone down here on this world pray things that are going to make any difference to God?" Well, just know this—people do! In James 5:16 it says very clearly, *". . . The effectual, fervent prayer of a righteous man availeth much."* I don't know how God handles that, but I know He does. He says, "You just pray, and I'll respond to your prayers." In 1 John 5:15 it says, *"And if we know that He hear us, whatever we ask, we know that we have the petitions that we desired of Him."* God promises to grant us what we pray for. Now there are some conditions that must be met to validate that promise, but we'll discuss that later.

Basically, then, we're to pray for several reasons: because God's going to answer if we pray, because it lines us up with God's purposes, because it puts God on display, because God told us to pray, and because it's a sin not to pray. So, there's good reason to pray.

QUESTION #2: *John, I know that the Bible says to pray without ceasing, but what does that mean? I've been compiling a prayer list which I go through at the end of the day, but could I be doing something better?*

I don't think you could be doing something better than having a prayer list and going through it at the end of the day, but when the Bible says, *"Pray without ceasing"* (1 Thess. 5:17), it is telling us not to restrict our life of prayer to a time period. There are many "religious groups" that have specified prayer hours. I've traveled in the Middle East where there are towers called minarets that summon everyone to prayer throughout the day. Those in Judaism had certain periods of time when they prayed, too. And we have the same perspective in many of our Protestant churches today. People go to church on Sunday, and that's their prayer time. Or they show up on Wednesday night for prayer meeting and they think that is the time to pray. But the Bible says, *"Pray without ceasing."* Prayer is to be a way of life.

A. Ceaseless Prayer Illustrated

I think the best way to illustrate this idea of ceaseless prayer is to compare it to breathing. You can't just breathe periodically and survive, can you? No. You have to breathe all the time. In fact, we live in an environment where the air pressure is such that it is easier to breathe than not to breathe. It's easier to breathe than to hold your breath, isn't it? When you hold your breath, you're fighting against the natural pressure of the air. Well, the same is true of prayer. We live in the environment of God's dimension where God is always exerting His influence on us. The easiest thing for us to do is to commune with His influence. So, when you don't pray, you're holding your breath spiritually. You're fighting against the very existence and presence of God in your life. Prayer, then, is to become a flow of life.

B. Ceaseless Prayer Defined

You say, "What does it mean to pray without ceasing?" Well, it doesn't mean to walk around with your eyes closed all the time, nor does it mean that all your prayers have to be forty-five minutes long. What it does mean, however, is that your heart should be open in constant communion with God. For example, have you ever been with a friend and felt tremendous communication, even though nothing had been said? Just realizing a person's presence oftentimes gives you a sense of communion, doesn't it? You don't necessarily have to be constantly talking to commune with someone.

Have you ever been away from a friend for a long time, without that friend ever leaving your mind? Well, it should be that way with God. We don't have to be constantly verbalizing—rattling off vain and endless repetition. Rather, we're to live with a constant awareness that He is present, and begin to see everything in the light of that presence. For example, if I'm with someone that I respect and love, and something happens to me that could make me angry, I do all I can to make sure that I don't get angry in front of that person I care about. Why? Because I'm sensitive to that friend's presence. In the spiritual dimension, that's what it means to pray without ceasing. We're to have such an open communion with God, that everything that happens in our lives is filtered through the fact that God is there with us.

We are able to constantly commune with God when we realize that He is always with us. For example, I was driving down the road recently, when I witnessed a police shoot-out. The police had surrounded a camper, and had their guns aimed at a man who was coming out of the camper with his arms up over his head. All I could think about, when I saw all of this taking place, was this guy's eternal soul, and whether or not he knew Christ. The whole scene was filtered through the grid of the presence of God with a perspective of how God would see it. That's communing with God—praying without ceasing.

So, I think it's great to have a prayer time set aside each day to pray for the needs of others. But that's not the end of it, it's only the beginning. In fact, maybe it's just the routine part of what ought to be a whole way of life. We're to be praying all the time . . . communing with God.

QUESTION #3: *How should we pray? Are there certain steps or formulas that we should follow?*

There aren't any formulas for prayer. Some people have thought that since Jesus gave us the Disciples' Prayer in Matthew 6:9-13, every time we pray we have to start out, *"Our Father, who art in heaven . . . ."* Do you know there's a group of people who believe that the only proper way to pray is to recite that particular prayer? In fact, they believe that praying anything else is a sin. Now that is not at all what Jesus was saying! He was simply giving a pattern for prayer—a skeletal outline to build upon. There are no formulas for prayer. There is nothing we can say to make God respond in a certain way. I do believe, however, that there are conditions that have to be met in prayer. They're not formulas—they're principles. Let me suggest them to you.

First of all, when we pray we must . . .

A. Ask in Christ's Name

We're back to the passage we looked at earlier in John 14. In verse 13 Jesus says, *"And whatever ye shall ask in My name, that will I do . . . ."* Then He repeats, in verse 14, *"If ye shall ask anything in My name, I will do it."*

1. THE CONFUSION

    Now, I don't know what that says to you, but some people think it means that you have to say, "In Jesus' name," before you say, "Amen." I was raised in a church that believed if someone prayed and just said amen at the end of his prayer, it never got beyond the ceiling. They believed that the formula, "In Jesus' name, amen," had to be at the end of every prayer. Otherwise, it wasn't an effective prayer. But that isn't what it means!

2. THE CLARIFICATION

    a. **The Significance of Christ's Name**

    What did Jesus mean when He said to pray in His name? Well, you have to understand how the word *name* is used in the Bible. It means "all that a person is." For example, in Exodus 3, when Moses asked God His name, God said, *"I AM THAT I AM"* (v. 14). In other words, "My name is who I am." So when Christ said to pray *"in My name,"* He was saying, "Pray prayers that are consistent with who I am—My person, My will, and My purposes." So the promise in John 14:13-14 is this: If you pray prayers that are consistent with the person and will of Jesus Christ, He'll hear and answer.

    b. **The Submission to Christ's Purposes**

    Now the question comes, "How do you know the purposes of Christ? How do you know the will of Christ? How do you know that you're praying in His name?" Well, in some cases you may not know, so you have to say, "Lord, Thy will be done. I don't know what Your will is in this case, but I ask that it might glorify Your name." In other cases, you *can* know the will of God. Let me show you:

    Before you approach the Lord in prayer the next time you think you need something, ask yourself if you can pray in the following way: "Lord, I really need a new car, a new wardrobe, a new girl friend, and anything else You can throw in. And I ask this because I know this is consistent with Jesus' name, purpose, and will." Now wait a minute. You don't know if that is really God's will, do you? No! You say, "But how *can* I know

God's will?" Well, how about going to God and saying, "God, I want to be the kind of Christian that You want me to be. I want to know Your power in my life. I want to know purity in my life. I want to be used to the maximum of my abilities. I want You to give me opportunities to preach the gospel to others. This I ask in the name of Jesus Christ because I believe it's consistent with His person and His work." Can you know whether or not those requests are according to God's will? Sure you can!

Your prayers, then, are to begin with an affirmation that you're asking in Jesus' name—lining yourself up with the will of God. So don't view "asking in Christ's name" as if it's some kind of a formula—some kind of a little magical ending you slap on the end of a prayer to make God responsible to answer it. Rather, see it as saying, "I only want this because I believe it is consistent with what I know about the will and work of the Lord Jesus Christ."

Through the years, in my own personal prayer life, I learned to always close my prayers with the following thought: "This I ask because I believe this is consistent with the will and the person of the Lord Jesus Christ." And since I know I'm coming to that at the end of my prayer, it has a way of filtering out some of the garbage along the way. So that's a very important condition in prayer. Let me give you another one:

B. Ask in Faith

In Matthew 21:22, Jesus said, *"And all things, whatever ye shall ask in prayer, believing, ye shall receive."* So, another element of prayer is that we have to ask in faith.

1. THE IMPORTANCE OF BELIEF

    We're to go to God with a sense of confidence because God wants to see us believe in Him. And I think the reason for that is this: When we trust God and He answers, we have cause to praise and glorify His name, and say, "God, You are worthy of our trust and confidence." Now, I don't think that God answers prayer primarily to prove to people that He's really there. In other words, if someone prays, "God, I don't know if You're there. And I really question whether or not You're involved in my life, or if You even care. But if You want to do something, go ahead." I don't think those are the biblical conditions in which God responds. Why? Because that's not somebody searching for faith, that's doubt looking for proof. What God responds to is one of His children who, like Abraham in Romans 4:20, *". . . staggered not at the promise of God through unbelief, but was strong in faith, giving glory to God."* God responds to a person who has faith, which builds the existing faith even stronger. So, God responds to us when we believe that He can hear and answer our prayer.

2. THE IMPLICATION OF UNBELIEF

If you don't believe God, the Bible says that you make Him a liar (1 Jn. 5:10). To say that God can't answer prayer or accomplish His will is to make Him a liar. As Christians, we dishonor God if we doubt Him. The world ought to be able to look at those of us who believe God and have confidence in Him and see people whose lives aren't falling apart. When the world hears someone who claims to be a Christian saying, "Oh, everything's going all wrong! Nothing's going right! I can't solve my problems! Where is God?" I'm sure they wonder what kind of a God Christians have.

So, God wants us to approach Him in strong faith. And if you have any questions about whether or not you can trust Him, all you have to do is go back to Scripture to see the past history of God answering the prayers of His people. That's the foundation for us to have faith that He'll answer our prayers. It also allows us to go on with life before the answer comes, because we believe that He'll give us the answer.

A third condition of prayer is that we are to . . .

C. Ask in God's Will

1. THE SPIRIT'S PRAYERS FOR US

In Romans 8:26 it says, "*. . . the Spirit also helpeth our infirmity* [or 'weakness']; *for we know not what we should pray for as we ought . . . .*" We don't know how to pray the way we ought to pray, do we? No, we really don't. We don't know the end from the beginning. For example, we don't know whether He wants to heal a person or whether He wants that person to die and go to heaven. We don't know whether He wants us to be in one particular ministry over another. And the examples are endless. So, sometimes we have to say, "Lord, I'm just waiting on You," because we don't know how to pray.

Later on in verse 26, we find out a marvelous thing. Since we don't know how to pray, "*. . . the Spirit Himself maketh intercession for us . . . .*" Isn't that great? The Spirit of God is interceding for us. We have an internal, resident Holy Spirit constantly praying for us. It's marvelous to realize that we have an intercessor in heaven—Christ the Son; and we have an intercessor here on earth—the Holy Spirit. Both are communing on our behalf with the Father.

The Holy Spirit, it says at the end of verse 26, is making intercession for us *"with groanings which cannot be uttered."* Now that's very simple to understand. These groanings can't be uttered; therefore, they can't be heard. They are unutterable groanings. You say, "Well, what are these groanings?" They are the language of the Spirit of God communing with the Father—strictly a divine language. Isn't it tremendous to realize that the Spirit of God is constantly praying for us?

Now, the key is in verse 27: *"And He [God the Father] that searcheth the hearts knoweth what is the mind of the Spirit, because He maketh intercession for the saints according to the will of God."* So, it's wonderful to realize that even when we don't know how to pray, the Spirit of God is always praying on our behalf, consistent with the will of God.

2. **OUR PRAYER IN THE SPIRIT**

In Ephesians 6:18, it says that we're to be *"praying . . . in the Spirit . . . ."* Now what does that mean? It simply means that since the Spirit is always praying in the will of God, we're to get lined up with Him. In other words, pray prayers that are consistent with the Spirit's prayers, so that in your prayer there's an underlying commitment that says, "I ask this only if this is Your will." Do you know what? I don't want one thing in my life that isn't in the will of God. Do you? I don't know about you, but I'm not ready for that kind of grief. Sometimes when we beg God for something that isn't His will, we get it. But it's no bargain! It usually becomes a lesson in learning to pray that God would give us only what is His will.

There's a fourth condition for prayer. We need to . . .

D. **Ask from a Pure Heart**

James 5:16 says: *". . . The effectual, fervent prayer of a righteous man availeth much."* That's another condition for prayer. There needs to be a righteous life. We have to ask from a pure heart. Now, what does it mean to be righteous? Well, there are two ways you can look at righteousness in the Bible. First of all, is the righteousness of Christ that is imputed to us when we become Christians. We literally take on the holiness of Christ. That's positional righteousness.

We are also to live righteously, aren't we? In other words, righteousness is also a practical issue. So in one sense, as Christians we are positionally righteous—we've been made right with God through Christ. But in another sense, we haven't quite lived up to who we really are in Christ. And I think what James is saying is that if we expect God to answer our prayers, there has to be a commitment to live a righteous life.

Now the word *"righteous"* means "right," that's all. You're to live right. If you're living right, God's going to hear your prayers. You know what it says in 1 Peter? It says that if you're married, your prayers will be hindered if your marriage relationship isn't right (1 Pet. 3:7). In other words, if things aren't right in your life at home, you're not meeting one of the conditions for prayer to be answered, to be beneficial to you, and to give glory to God.

Let me give you another principle. A fifth condition of prayer is that you . . .

E. Ask in Earnestness

Luke 11:5-10 gives us a most fascinating story—a parable from our Lord. Look at what it says: *"And He said unto them, Which of you shall have a friend, and shall go unto him at midnight, and say unto him, Friend, lend me three loaves; for a friend of mine in his journey is come to me, and I have nothing to set before him? And he, from within, shall answer, and say, Trouble me not; the door is now shut, and my children are with me in bed* [for warmth, no doubt]; *I cannot rise and give thee. I say unto you, Though he will not rise and give him because he is his friend, yet because of his importunity* [i.e., his continuous banging] *he will rise and give him as many as he needeth. And I say unto you, Ask, and it shall be given you; seek, and ye shall find; knock, and it shall be opened unto you."*

Now, what's Jesus' point? He's saying that we're to pray with earnestness. God's not up in heaven saying, "Knock a little harder!" That's not the idea. What He's saying is that we ought to have such a tremendous concern for someone else's needs, that we bring those needs to God with earnestness. Do you remember when Jacob wrestled with the Lord, and wouldn't let go till he got a blessing (Gen. 32:24-30)? I think we need to have that kind of persistence and earnestness—not to try and force God to do something, but to demonstrate to God the heart of compassion and the genuineness of a concerned and caring soul.

It's so easy for us to pray in a glib way. I remember one time when I was praying with my little daughter, Melinda. Her prayer went something like this: "God bless the whole wide world. Amen." I said, "What kind of a prayer was that? God can't bless the whole wide world. That's too nonspecific. It doesn't demonstrate any individual compassion and care. You need to be concerned about individual people in the whole wide world, and then take *them* to the Lord." Well, we had a good little discussion about what it means to pray more specifically so that we can pray in earnestness.

One more condition of prayer is that we must . . .

F. Ask with Awareness

When we pray, we should be aware of what is going on around us. Several places in the Gospels, Jesus said to *"watch and pray"* (e.g., Mt. 26:41; Mk. 13:33; 14:38; Lk. 21:36). And in 1 Peter 4:7, Peter said to *"watch unto prayer."* In other words, we're to pray in response to what we see going on. Keep your eyes open, and be alert to spiritual needs. Be sensitive to what's going on, and out of your watchfulness, you'll know how to pray.

QUESTION #4: *John, what should the content of our prayers consist of?*

That's a good question. Once you've met all the conditions of prayer—you're earnest, you're aware, your heart's right, you're pure, you're asking in Christ's name, and you're lined up with God's will—what do you say? In other words, what are the elements of prayer? Well, the first element of prayer is . . .

A. Confession of Sin

1. THE PATTERN OF CONFESSION

    I think the greatest prayer in the Old Testament is in Daniel 9. It's a model of prayer, particularly in terms of confession. Now, if ever there was someone who was right before God, it was Daniel. He was an uncompromising man of God. Though he lived in a pagan society, he consistently lived a pure life. But even such a man as Daniel talked about his sin when he came before the Lord. And if he wasn't confessing his own sin, he so identified with the people around him, that he confessed their sin.

    In verses 3-6 of chapter 9, Daniel says, *"And I set my face unto the Lord God, to seek by prayer and supplications, with fasting, and sackcloth, and ashes; and I prayed unto the LORD, my God, and made my confession . . . ."* Whenever you go into the presence of God, you have to sense the fact that you are a sinner coming to a holy God. That's why prayer should begin with confession of sin. Continuing on in verse 4, Daniel says, *". . . [I] made my confession, and said, O Lord, the great and awesome God, keeping the covenant and mercy to them that love Him, and to them that keep His commandments, we have sinned, and have committed iniquity, and have done wickedly, and have rebelled, even by departing from Thy precepts and from Thine ordinances; neither have we hearkened unto Thy servants, the prophets . . . ."*

Daniel goes on like this through verse 15. Then in verse 16 he says, *"O Lord, according to all Thy righteousness, I beseech Thee, let Thine anger and Thy fury be turned away . . . ."* You see, when you go into the presence of God, you have to realize that the only reason you can do that and come out alive is God's great grace and mercy. Lamentations 3:22 says, *"It is because of the LORD's mercies that we are not consumed . . . ."* So, I believe that prayer begins with confession.

2. THE PURPOSE OF CONFESSION

   a. ***It Eliminates Improper Requests***

   It's a healthy thing to begin our prayers with confession of sin, because it reminds us that we don't deserve anything. It helps us eliminate certain things on our checklist. Sometimes when we pray, we rush in and say, "Hey, Lord, it's me again. I'm one of Your children, I've been going to church, and I've been reading my Bible. I'm a basically holy person. So, Lord, there ought to be a few favors up there that you can send my way." Well, all that gets eliminated when you enter the presence of God with the brokenness and the contrite heart of one who confesses his sin. When you affirm to God that you don't deserve anything, you eliminate any self-centeredness in your prayer.

   There's a lot of talk today about the fact that we should demand things from God, and that He has to give us what we ask. But you won't have that perspective if you go into the presence of God with a broken and a contrite heart. In Isaiah 66:2, the Lord says that He seeks *"him that is poor and of a contrite spirit, and trembleth at My word."* If when you pray, you go in trembling at your own sinfulness, and you confess to God your weaknesses and failures, it will filter your prayer life considerably. Your prayers will then sound something like this: "Lord, I really don't deserve anything; I just want to see Your will done." Then you can tell Him what is on your heart.

   Another reason it's important to confess our sin is . . .

   b. ***It Eliminates Thoughts of Unjust Chastening***

   One great reason why it's important to confess our sin is so that God can chasten us without being thought unfair. When we sin, God chastens to correct us, right? Well, if we've already confessed that sin, we will not think that He's unjust when He chastens us. That's very important.

Do you remember the story of Achan in Joshua 7? He stole from the spoils of the conquered city of Jericho, which was specifically forbidden by Joshua. In verse 19, Joshua confronted Achan and said, *". . . give, I pray thee, glory to the LORD God of Israel, and make confession unto Him . . . ."* Joshua told him to confess his sin. Why? Because before God destroyed Achan and his whole family, God wanted to be sure that Achan had told the whole world that he was deserving of the judgment he was going to get. So, one of the reasons that we confess our sin is to free God to chasten us without our having any thoughts of Him being unjust, or unfair, or unloving, or unmerciful.

Now, when God does chasten us, it's for our good, isn't it? Hebrews 12:5-11 says that He chastens us as sons so that we might be better sons. He certainly should never be accused, in a negative way, for doing that. I've heard people say, "My life isn't going right! What kind of a God would do this to me? I don't understand why God's treating me this way . . . I thought He loved me." Listen, if you're involved in confessing your sin, you're not going to be talking about God like that. Instead, you're going to see that God is using those things to shape you, and to draw you away from sin to the things that are right. So, confession is critical.

Let me give you a second important element of the content of prayer:

B. Praise

Praise is very important. Psalm 50:23 says, *"Whoso offereth praise glorifieth Me . . . ."* First Thessalonians 5:18 says, *"In everything give thanks . . . ."* Of the many psalms that are prayers, there are far more psalms of praise than psalms of petition. Why? Because the psalmist was involved in praising God.

Now, what does it mean to praise God? How do we praise the Lord? Let me give you three elements of praise:

1. RECITE GOD'S ATTRIBUTES

We give God praise when we recite His attributes. In Habakkuk 1:13, Habakkuk said, *"Thou art of purer eyes than to behold evil, and canst not look on iniquity . . . ."* Then he went on to talk about the covenant-keeping God, the almighty God, the God of promise, and so forth. That's praising God—reciting all of His characteristics and attributes. So when you pray, you want to say, "God, You're a God of love, a God of glory, a God of grace, a God of majesty, a God of mercy, and a God of wisdom." You see, that's praise!

A second element of praise is to . . .

2. RECITE GOD'S WORKS

As you recite the things God has done, you are affirming that God is worthy to be praised. Many of the psalms do this. They basically say, "Thou art the God who delivered the children of Israel. Thou art the God that parted the Red Sea. Thou art the God that did this, and Thou art the God that did that" . . . and so on. Then, after you've talked about what a great God you have and what great things He has done, it's not hard to say, "Lord, I have this quiz tomorrow . . . do You think You can handle it?" Praise bolsters your confidence in God because of all the great things He's done in the past. So, when you go to the Lord with a problem, if you've given Him praise first, it's easy to say, "Lord, with all that You've done, I'm sure You can handle my problem, too."

After you've recited all His attributes, and you've recited all His works, another important thing to do is to . . .

3. SAY THANKS

When I'm done reciting God's attributes and works, I say thanks. I say, "Thank You, God, for being the God that You are, and doing the things You do." I'm thankful that such a great God, who does such great things, is a God who personally works in my own life.

The third element in the content of prayer is . . .

C. Petition

1. THE ORIGIN OF THE WORD

Another word for petition is *supplication*. The Greek word translated *supplication*, originally meant "to bring an olive branch to a sovereign." If you wanted a favor from the king, you'd bow down before him and offer him an olive branch, which served as a peace offering. Only then could you give him your request. In a similar way, when you come to God with supplication, you come into the presence of the King, you kneel before Him, you offer Him an olive branch, and you ask Him your petition. God wants to hear what's on your heart. You don't need to be afraid to do that. He wants to hear the cry of your heart, the petition of your heart, the thing that you desire.

2. THE OBJECTS OF PETITION

The petitions that you offer to God can be on behalf of . . .

a. **Ourselves**

I believe that God wants to hear about you. I believe that that should be a part of our petition. Philippians 4:6 indicates this when it says, *"Be anxious for nothing, but in everything, by prayer and supplication with thanksgiving, let your requests be made known unto God."* We shouldn't be anxious over things in our own life because we're to take them to God in prayer. In 1 Peter 5:7 it says, *"Casting all your care upon Him; for He careth for you."*

Not only are we to petition God on behalf of ourselves, we're also to petition God on behalf of . . .

b. **Others**

We're to be praying for others. In Ephesians 6:18 it says, *"Praying always with all prayer and supplication . . . for all saints."*

So, we're to go to God with confession, with praise, and with petition. That's the content of prayer.

QUESTION #5: *John, is there anything we do, or don't do, that keeps our prayers from being answered?*

That's an important thing to know, isn't it? So, let's look at what hinders our prayers.

A. Generally

First of all, what generally hinders prayer? Sin. There's no question about that. We know that sin hinders prayer. Psalm 66:18 is a good verse to remember. It says, *"If I regard iniquity in my heart, the Lord will not hear me."* Sin puts a barrier in front of prayer. But that's general. Let's look at what hinders prayer . . .

B. Specifically

1. SELFISHNESS

   James 4:3 says, *"Ye ask, and receive not, because ye ask amiss, that ye may consume it upon your lusts."* That's the first hindrance to prayer—selfishness. Listen, we don't go to God just to get things for ourselves. Don't ever pray, "Lord, I want this, and I don't care what it does to Your Kingdom, or Your name, or anybody else's either." You can't pray like that and get anywhere with God! That's not how you get things from God, that's how you *don't* get things from Him.

2. UNCONCERN

A second thing that hinders prayer is unconcern or indifference. This hindrance to prayer comes from a principle out of the Old Testament. In Proverbs 21:13 it says, *"Whoso stoppeth his ears at the cry of the poor, he also shall cry himself, but shall not be heard."* In other words, if you can close up your concern for somebody else, God can close up His concern for you. And we're back, again, to the problem of selfishness, aren't we? So when we pray, we want to make sure that we're not indifferent to the needs of those around us. Our prayers should reflect the following attitude: "Lord, fit my request into the whole picture, so that in giving to me, no one else will lose out." So, don't pray for yourself as if you were isolated from the rest of God's people.

3. AN UNFORGIVING SPIRIT

I believe that prayer is hindered by an unforgiving spirit. That's another specific sin that the Bible says can hinder prayer. There are several places in Scripture that support this, but let's look at Mark 11:25. It says this: *"And when ye stand praying, forgive, if ye have anything against any, that your Father also, who is in heaven, may forgive you your trespasses."* So when you get up to pray, make sure you've forgiven anyone who has offended you. Now, if you haven't forgiven someone, Matthew 5:23-24 says that you better leave that place, go to that person, and get things right. Then you can come back. You can't worship God if you're holding something against somebody in your heart. You're asking God to pour out all of His love, all of His mercy, and all of His grace on you—an undeserving sinner who won't forgive and be gracious to another undeserving sinner. So you're asking from God something you won't do yourself.

In Matthew 18:23-35, Jesus told the parable of a king who called in all of his servants to give him a report. When he found out that one of his servants owed him a fortune, that servant pleaded with the king and told him that he would pay everything back. Instead of requiring that the servant pay everything back, the king forgave him everything. Well, that servant went straight to someone who owed him eighteen dollars, grabbed him by the throat, and demanded payment. When he didn't get it, the unforgiving servant threw him in prison. Well, we're just as inconsistent. We go to God and want everything that He can give to us. But at the same time, we're carrying a grudge against somebody. Now, if God is going to be gracious to us, He'll be gracious when He sees us being gracious to someone else.

4. HOME PROBLEMS

    Another hindrance to prayer is problems in the home. First Peter 3:7 says that you better make sure things are right in your marriage relationship so *"that your prayers be not hindered."* When there's conflict in the home, the clear channel of God's answers to prayer is directly confused.

5. DOUBT

    James 1:5-7 says, *"If any of you lack wisdom, let him ask of God, who giveth to all men liberally, and upbraideth not* [holds back nothing], *and it shall be given him. But let him ask in faith, nothing wavering. For he that wavereth is like a wave of the sea driven with the wind and tossed. For let not that man think that he shall receive anything of the Lord."* In other words, if you go to God wavering between believing and not believing, doubt becomes a barrier to God giving you what He wants. Why? Because He wants your complete trust.

So, those are some of the things that hinder prayer. Fortunately, I think we can deal with all of them in one act—beginning all of our prayers with confession. Then once we get the channel clean, we can go on to the praise and the petition.

Well, I hope this helps in your prayer life—not so much for your sake, but for the sake of the glory of God.

Focusing on the Facts

1. What does it mean that we can cry *"Abba, Father"* (Rom. 8:15b)? Why is this significant? (see p. 23)

2. What are the five reasons we are to pray? (see pp. 23-27)

3. What is our responsibility, according to Ephesians 6:18? What does the context of this verse tell you about its importance? (see pp. 23-24)

4. What is a paradox? Give some biblical examples. How are we to respond to paradoxes in Scripture? What is the danger in trying to harmonize a paradox? (see pp. 24-25)

5. Why should we pray, according to 1 Samuel 12:23? (see p. 25)

6. How does prayer give glory to God? (see pp. 25-26)

7. When we pray, should we be more interested in telling God what we want, or in asking God what He wants? Why? (see pp. 26-27)

8. Give some scriptural references to support the fact that God *does* answer prayer. (see p. 27)

9. What does it mean to *"pray without ceasing"* (1 Thess. 5:17)? What's a good way to illustrate that concept? (see p. 28)

10. What was Jesus' purpose in giving the Disciples' Prayer in Matthew 6:9-13? (see p. 29)

11. Is a prayer ineffective if it is not ended with the phrase, "In Jesus' name. Amen."? What does it mean to pray in Christ's name? (see p. 30)

12. How can we know if we're praying according to the will of God? (see pp. 30-31)

13. According to Matthew 21:22, what is an important condition to answered prayer? Why is this important? What implication can be made if this condition isn't met? (see p. 31)

14. When God responds to a prayer of faith, what happens in that person's life as a result? (see p. 32)

15. What's a good thing to do when you find your faith in God wavering? (see p. 32)

16. What ministry does the Holy Spirit have in a Christian's life as it relates to prayer? Why does He need to do this? (see p. 32)

17. What does it mean to be *"praying . . . in the Spirit"* (Eph. 6:18)? (see p. 33)

18. Explain the difference between positional and practical righteousness. Which of these is referred to in James 5:16 as a condition for effective prayer? (see p. 33)

19. Jesus uses a parable in Luke 11:5-10 to teach what important principle of prayer? (see p. 34)

20. What does it mean to be earnest in prayer? (see p. 34)

21. What phrase did Jesus use in the Gospels to encourage us to pray with an awareness of the needs around us? (see p. 35)

22. What are the three major elements that make up the content of prayer? (see pp. 35-36)

23. When we pray, why is it a good idea to always start by confessing our sin? (see p. 36)

24. How does our response to God's chastening change, once we've confessed the sin we're being chastened for? (see p. 36)

25. What are the three elements of praise? (see pp. 37-38)

26. What is the original meaning of the Greek word for *supplication*? How does this apply to our petitioning God in prayer? (see p. 38)

27. Are we ever to petition God on behalf of ourselves? Explain. (see p. 39)

28. The Bible mentions five specific sins that will hinder our prayers. What are they? (see pp. 39-41)

Pondering the Principles
(For Group Discussion)

1. What would you say to another Christian who felt that since God is sovereign and will accomplish His own will, there's no reason for us to pray?
2. Why must we obey the commands of Scripture whether or not we understand or agree with them?
3. What are the effects in a Christian's life when God answers prayer? What do you think is the primary reason that God answers prayer? Why should we be involved in actively looking for needs to pray about?
4. How would you explain to someone why we're not to limit our time of prayer to before meals and before we go to bed at night? What are some practical ways to cultivate an attitude of constant prayer?
5. Do you think that the Disciples' Prayer in Matthew 6:9-13 (also known as the Lord's Prayer) should be a part of your daily prayer life? Should it be routinely prayed in a Sunday worship service? Explain your answers.
6. How can you be certain that you are praying according to God's will?
7. What are some practical steps that we can take to increase our faith in God's ability to answer prayer? What are some good ways to teach our children the meaning of faith and to develop them into men and women of faith?
8. Why do we need to be aware of what is going on in the world around us? What are the best ways to gain this awareness? How are you personally applying Peter's exhortation in 1 Peter 4:7? If you aren't applying it, what steps can you take to begin to apply it?
9. If you were in the habit of neglecting to confess your sins, how would you tend to approach God in prayer? What effect would it have on your perspective of the chastening of God in your life?
10. What is praise? When you pray, do you always give God praise? What are some specific things that you can praise God for right now?
11. What are the three basic elements of prayer? Of the three, which one do you think is the most important? Why?
12. Psalm 66:18 tells us that unconfessed sin hinders our prayers. The Bible also mentions five specific sins that hinder our prayers. What are they? Which ones do you have the most trouble with? What steps can you take to gain victory over those particular sins which you are prone to commit?

Selected Scriptures   Tape GC 2032

HOW TO FELLOWSHIP

Introduction

One of the basic concepts of the Christian life is fellowship. So far in this series, we've talked about prayer and we've talked about how to study the Bible. Let's look, now, at the idea of fellowship and how it relates to the definition of the church.

QUESTION #1: *With all the different denominations in Christianity, can we really say we're one body? What is the basis for our fellowship?*

People say, "I belong to this fellowship," or "I belong to that fellowship," and "We don't fellowship with those folks because they cross their *t* and dot their *i* differently." Well, there's a real problem with Christians getting together on a common basis, isn't there? Let's take a look, then, at . . .

A. The Basis for Fellowship

John, in referring to his experience with Christ, said this: *"That which we have seen and heard declare we unto you* [Christ and His gospel], *that ye also may have fellowship with us; and truly our fellowship is with the Father, and with His Son, Jesus Christ. And these things write we unto you, that your joy may be full"* (1 Jn. 1:3-4). Now, since our fellowship is with God the Father and His Son Jesus Christ, if you know God and you know Christ, you're in the fellowship. The fellowship is not a group of people who all believe one little thing about a certain rather obscure truth, nor is the fellowship made up of people who all come from one ethnic background, one part of the country, or one theological heritage. The fellowship is not even based upon which method one uses to baptize. Though many of those things are important, our fellowship is with the Father and with His Son, Jesus Christ. So, the basis of fellowship, as you look at it in a foundational sense, is that we know Jesus Christ. I may not agree with your interpretation of an obscure passage of Scripture, and you may differ on some minor point of doctrine, but I have to admit that if you know Jesus Christ, and you know God the Father, you're in the fellowship.

B. The Building of Fellowship

The word *fellowship*, in the Greek, is *koinōnia*. It comes from the verb *koinōneō*, which means "to be partners." So if you're a Christian, you're a partner.

1. OUR JOINING TO THE LORD

   In 1 Corinthians 6:17, Paul made the following statement: *"But he that is joined unto the Lord is one spirit."* When you became a Christian you were joined to the Lord, weren't you? Romans 6:3-4 tells us that we were united with Him in His death, and united with Him in His resurrection. Therefore, we are to *"walk in newness of life."* In Galatians 2:20 Paul said, *"I am crucified with Christ: nevertheless I live; yet not I, but Christ liveth in me . . . ."* We are joined to the Lord.

2. OUR JOINING TO EACH OTHER

   Now, if we're all joined to the Lord, then we're also all joined to one another, right? So the truth of fellowship is that all who are saved are in the fellowship. Instead of isolating ourselves into little groups and saying, "They don't believe everything that I believe, they don't think the way I think, and they don't do what I do," we need to get together. Why? Because we can rub the rough edges off one another and help each other to understand things more clearly. Maybe some of the folks who disagree with us need our input on something . . . and maybe we need their input, too. And the more time we spend together around the things of God—stimulating, provoking, exhorting, and considering one another—the more we'll be channeled by the Spirit of God into real oneness and fellowship.

   So, at the very beginning, we have to say that anybody who knows Jesus Christ is a partner with us. And since we'll be partners forever, it would be nice if we could start getting along while we're down here. Why? Because Jesus said, *"By this shall all men know that ye are My disciples, if ye have love one to another"* (Jn. 13:35). Our testimony, then, is at stake in this whole concept of fellowship.

C. **The Barrier to Fellowship**

Now, it's important to see beyond some of the artificial and traditional barriers that have been in the way of our fellowship, but sometimes there are real barriers to fellowship. For example, if someone has unconfessed sin in his life, I can't fellowship with him, in the fullest sense, because his life isn't the way it ought to be. We'll look at this in more detail later (see pp. 51-52).

Basically, then, salvation puts us into the fellowship. So when you see people in church who look like they don't understand what's going on in the world and they look like they are spiritually out of it, remember that because they are one with the Lord, and because you are one with the Lord, you are one with each other. They need you, and you need them, right? That's what fellowship is . . . and that's the way we have to see it.

QUESTION #2: *John, is there a good example of fellowship in the Bible?*

Yes, there is! Let's go all the way back to the first church in Acts 2, and see what the fellowship was like when it was just beginning. In Acts 2, we find that the church was born on the Day of Pentecost when the Spirit of God was poured out on one hundred and twenty disciples in the upper room. These disciples went out and miraculously declared the wonderful works of God—in languages they had never learned—to unbelieving Jews who had gathered in Jerusalem for Passover. Then Peter preached a great sermon in Acts 2:14-36, where three thousand people were converted, baptized, and added to the church. That infant church, which had not yet been affected by the world and cluttered by the process of history, was perhaps the purest church. So, if we want to see the characteristics of real fellowship, we need to look at the characteristics of that first church in Acts 2:42-47.

The first characteristic of a fellowshiping church is that . . .

A. It Is Sharing (v. 42)

1. THE SHARING OF TRUTH

    "And they continued steadfastly in the apostles' doctrine . . ."

    The early church met together regularly and studied the Apostles' doctrine, which was the inspired doctrine of the New Covenant. Fellowship, then, has to include a sharing of truth—people coming together and sharing the truth about God.

2. THE SHARING OF MINISTRY

    "And they continued steadfastly in . . . fellowship . . ."

    I believe the word *"fellowship"* here means "mutual ministry." They were mutually sharing in ministry with one another. For example, if you needed prayer, I'd pray for you. If you needed wisdom, I'd give you that wisdom. If you needed assistance, I'd assist you. I would help with whatever spiritual ministry that I could render to you. That's part of fellowship.

3. THE SHARING OF THE LORD'S TABLE

    "And they continued steadfastly . . . in breaking of bread . . ."

    The phrase *"breaking of bread"* refers to the celebration of the Lord's Table. Fellowship for the early church involved coming together around the Lord's Table and sharing the burden of each other's sin. In other words, they were holding each other up, as Galatians 6:1-2 says, *"Brethren,*

> *if a man be overtaken in a fault, ye who are spiritual restore such an one in the spirit of meekness, considering thyself, lest thou also be tempted. Bear ye one another's burdens . . . ."*

So I think they shared teaching, they shared ministry, and they even shared in the bearing of the burden of sin.

4. THE SHARING OF PRAYER

"And they continued steadfastly . . . in prayers."

The early church shared in the matter of prayer—coming before the Lord in confession, petition, and praise.

So, the essence of fellowship, if we were to distill it down to one concept, is that it is a sharing experience. It's people coming together on the common ground of salvation in Jesus Christ, to mutually give back and forth to each other those things that are most needful. And what is most needful? That we share the truth; that we share our ministries; that we share in the Lord's Table, in the sense that we affirm each other and hold each other up when we fall; and that we share together in prayer.

A second characteristic of a fellowshiping church is that . . .

B. It Is Filled with Awe (v. 43a)

"And fear came upon every soul . . ."

The fear being referred to here is a sense of awe. You say, "Why were they in awe?" Because a church that is sharing the way they were sharing, is going to see God at work in their midst. The power of God was so evident among them, that the people lived in a state of awe.

A third thing that characterizes a fellowshiping church is that . . .

C. It Is Powerful (v. 43b)

". . . and many wonders and signs were done by the apostles."

There was a freedom for the power of God to flow. In Matthew 13, Jesus returned to His hometown of Nazareth, but *"He did not many mighty works there because of their unbelief"* (v. 58). Well, that certainly wasn't true in this church. There was such an affirmation of the things of God, and such a free flow of the Holy Spirit's power, that the leadership was able to see God accomplish all the things that they wanted.

A fourth characteristic of a fellowshiping church is that . . .

D. It Is United (v. 44a)

"And all that believed were together . . ."

That's a great statement, isn't it? Everybody was together. They were all one in the Spirit . . . in the truest sense. Unfortunately, by the time you move out of the book of Acts into the book of 1 Corinthians, you find a church that doesn't have unity. The Corinthian church was so disconnected and disjointed, that Paul had to write them and say, *"Now I beseech you, brethren, by the name of our Lord Jesus Christ, that ye all speak the same thing, and that there be no divisions among you, but that ye be perfectly joined together in the same mind and in the same judgment"* (1 Cor. 1:10). To the Philippians he wrote, *". . . be like-minded, having the same love, being of one accord, of one mind"* (2:2).

Even before we get out of the New Testament, the church has already lost its sense of real unity. But the first church, here in Acts 2, was characterized by unity . . . pure togetherness. They were all together and committed to each other.

A fifth characteristic of a fellowshiping church is that . . .

E. It Is Caring (vv. 44b-45)

    1. SHARING AVAILABLE RESOURCES (v. 44b)

       "And all that believed . . . had all things common"

       Do you know what that means? Everybody had a right to everybody else's resources. For example, I don't feel that I own anything. I only manage things for God. So, if you need what I have more than I need it, it's yours. Why? Because it all belongs to the Lord. We all need to get to the point in our Christian life where we know we don't possess anything, we just manage it. We're not owners, we're just stewards. Who owns everything? God does. He's given it to us to manage and to use for His glory. Well, that's the way this church in Acts 2 was. If somebody had a need, they met it. If you had the resources, and someone else had a need, your resources were for his need. And the same was true if you had a need—somebody else's resources would be for you.

       Now, not only did they have all things common, they were also . . .

    2. SELLING TO MEET NEEDS (v. 45)

       "And sold [lit. 'were selling'] *their possessions and goods, and parted* [lit. 'were parting'] *them to all men, as every man had need."*

       Notice that they didn't sell all their goods all at one time. It wasn't some kind of Christian communism, where everybody sold everything and then doled the earnings out equally. No, they were always in the process of selling their possessions as the needs arose. If everybody had just sold everything, pooled all the money, and then distributed it so that everybody had an equal share, it wouldn't have worked. Why? Because then there would be no need for anybody to minister to anyone else. In order to have people ministering to one another, there must be some "have-nots" and some "haves," right? So, as people had needs, other people sold their possessions to meet those needs. It was a marvelous demonstration of what it means to really care for others.

A sixth characteristic of a fellowshiping church is that . . .

F. It Is Dynamic (vv. 46-47)

"And they, continuing daily with one accord in the temple, and breaking bread from house to house, did eat their food with gladness and singleness of heart, praising God, and having favor with all the people. And the Lord added to the church daily such as should be saved."

This church had a testimony that couldn't be refuted. They were so dynamic in the world, because of their loving unity and fellowship, that the Lord added new converts to the church daily. People were coming to Christ because of the tremendous testimony of their fellowship.

That's the essence of fellowship. We can talk about fellowship being a theological and spiritual reality for all Christians, but it doesn't work itself out practically unless there's a real sharing. That's the heart and soul of fellowship.

QUESTION #3: *John, what role does the Lord's Table play in the true meaning of fellowship?*

The best way to understand what role the Lord's Table plays in our fellowship is to look at 1 Corinthians 10 and 11. First of all, according to 1 Corinthians 10, the Lord's Table is . . .

A. The Symbol of Our Fellowship

1. IT CELEBRATES OUR UNITY WITH CHRIST

    In 1 Corinthians 10:16 it says, *"The cup of blessing which we bless, is it not the communion of the blood of Christ? The bread which we break, is it not the communion of the body of Christ?"* Now that's an amazing statement! What he's saying is this: "When you come together and take the cup and the bread, in a very real sense you are fellowshiping with Christ Himself." When we participate in the Lord's Table, I believe that Christ is right there celebrating with us. The fact that we come to His Table with Him, is a marvelous concept. Now, I don't think we should look at this mystically. We should look at it in the same way that we sense the Lord's communion with us when we sing His praises and read His Word. When we come to the Lord's Table, His presence is there ministering in a wonderful, spiritual, supernatural way.

So, when we come to the Table and take the cup and the bread, we are acknowledging the presence of the living Lord Jesus Christ and communing with Him. That's why I believe that the Lord's Table is so very important to true fellowship.

A second reason that the Lord's Table is a symbol of our fellowship is . . .

2. IT CELEBRATES OUR UNITY WITH EACH OTHER

All distinctions are eliminated at the Lord's Table and we automatically become one. This unity occurs in two ways. First of all, we become one as we recognize . . .

a. **Our Common Sinfulness**

We're all sinners, right? All of us had to have the blood of Christ cover our sins, didn't we? That eliminates all distinctions! No one is better than anyone else at the Lord's Table. All of us needed the same sacrifice by Jesus Christ to deliver us from our sin. There's a tremendous common ground for unity in the recognition of that truth—sweeping away all distinction.

Did you know that there are people in the church of Jesus Christ who sometimes get the idea that they're better than other people in the church of Jesus Christ? They even become self-righteous and haughty. Let's face it, though, we get those ideas, too. We don't mean to, but it still happens nevertheless. We look down on someone else because we think our sins are more sophisticated than theirs. But when we come to the Lord's Table, we're forced to acknowledge the fact that we all needed the blood of Jesus Christ, and we're saying, "My sin was so severe that it required Christ's death. No one else's sin was any more severe than mine, so no one else required a greater act on the part of Christ than I did." So, there's a great commonness when we realize we're all sinners.

Our unity at the Lord's Table also occurs when we recognize . . .

b. **_Our Common Salvation_**

>The flip side of realizing that we are all sinners is realizing that we've all been saved in the same way. So, we're all one in that sense, too. We possess the same salvation and the same eternal life. We all have the same life of God within us. It's no different in you than it is in me, although God marvelously and wonderfully manifests Himself in unique ways.

So, I believe that coming to the Lord's Table is a very critical time; but not only because it is a symbol of our fellowship. The Lord's Table is also important in eliminating . . .

B. The Barrier to Our Fellowship

It is important for us to deal with sin when we come to the Lord's Table, because sin is the thing that breaks the fellowship.

1. SIN'S EXAMINATION

   In 1 Corinthians 11:28, it says that before we can come to the Lord's Table we have to examine ourselves. We have to confess our sins, or else sin will put a barrier into the fellowship that we should be celebrating. Sin is a tremendous hindrance to fellowship. In fact, it destroys the fellowship.

2. SIN'S EFFECT

   In 1 Corinthians 11:27-31, Paul discusses the fact that some people in the church were weak, some people were sickly, and some people had actually died, because they came to the Lord's Table with sin in their lives, pretending that everything was okay. Well, the Lord actually took the lives of some of those people. You know, it isn't too farfetched to believe that some of the people in the church whom we think died because they got sick physically, died because the Lord took them out of the church for desecrating or violating His Table. It's a time, then, that we must focus on sin.

3. SIN'S ELIMINATION

   Now if sin destroys our fellowship, then you can see why the Lord's Table is so important. The confession that occurs eliminates the barrier to fellowship. I want to encourage all of you who love the Lord Jesus Christ, to go to the Lord's Table regularly. Jesus said, *". . . this do in remembrance of Me"* (Lk. 22:19b). And Paul said, *"For as often as ye eat this bread, and drink this cup, ye do show the Lord's death till He come"* (1 Cor. 11:26).

So, why are you to participate in the Lord's Table regularly? Because when you examine yourself, the Spirit of God reveals your sin. Once you deal with your sin and set it aside, the fellowship can come together. That's why Jesus told His disciples that if they had something against somebody, they had to take care of it before they could worship (Mt. 5:23-24). In other words, you have to be dealing with sin in order for fellowship to be all that it should be.

QUESTION #4: *Now that we know what fellowship is, how do we put it into practice?*

Putting flesh to our fellowship falls into two general categories: spiritual gifts and mutual ministry. First let's look at . . .

A. Spiritual Gifts

1. THE SINGULARITY

    Romans 12, 1 Corinthians 12, and Ephesians 4:11-12 talk about certain gifts that every believer has been given. However, a very important statement is made in 1 Peter 4:10-11 that I want you to see: *"As every man hath received the gift, even so minister the same one to another, as good stewards of the manifold grace of God. If any man speak, let him speak as the oracles of God; if any man minister, let him do it as of the ability which God giveth . . . ."* Now, the statement I want you to see is in verse 10, where Peter says that every man has received *the* gift. The context shows that he's talking about spiritual gifts. So, when you were saved, I believe that you were given one spiritual gift. You say, "I thought we were given many spiritual gifts." Well, Peter used a singular noun when he said that every man had received *the* gift. That's only one reason why I believe each one of us has only one spiritual gift. I'll show you more reasons as we look at . . .

2. THE SPECIFICS

    You say, "Okay, so I've been given a spiritual gift. What's a spiritual gift?" A spiritual gift is a Holy-Spirit-empowered ability to minister to the body.

    a. ***The Gifts Categorized***

    The spiritual gifts are listed in 1 Corinthians 12 and Romans 12. Included in those lists are some miraculous sign gifts which were particularly for the Apostolic Age, but the church is still dependent on all the other gifts. We need people with the gift of helps, don't we? We need people with the gift of showing mercy to those in need. We need people with the gift of giving. We need people with the gift of teaching, the gift of preaching, the gift of leadership, and all of the other gifts.

Now, I believe that all of those gifts are simply *categories* of giftedness. Take the gift of teaching, for example. Have you ever noticed that people who are gifted in teaching, all teach differently? They all have different styles and emphases, don't they? You say, "Well, how can that be the same gift then?" Because the gift of teaching is a category of giftedness, and within that category is tremendous diversity. And the same thing applies to all the gifts. In 1 Corinthians 12:4-6, the Apostle Paul talks about the *"diversities of gifts,"* the *"differences of administrations,"* and the *"diversities of operations."* In other words, all the gifts come in different packages.

b. **The Gifts Combined**

Taking it a step further, I believe that the Lord selects elements out of all the categories of spiritual gifts, and puts them together in your own unique gift. In other words, your spiritual gift is not one gift out of one category, it's a combination of categories blended together to make you into a spiritual snowflake. There are no two of you alike. When your spiritual gift is blended together with your personality and capabilities, and when you are endowed and empowered by the Spirit of God, you can do something in the body of Christ that nobody else can do, in the way that only you can do it. That's why you're a critical part of the body of Christ. We're not rubber ducks that have been stamped out on an assembly line so that we all quack the same way. Each of us has a unique blending together of gifts.

For example, when I look at my own life, I know that God has called me to teach His Word, so I must have some element of the teaching gift. He's called me to shepherd in His church, so I must have some giftedness in the area of leadership, right? And I also feel that I might have a little of the gift of knowledge (the ability to understand the Word), because I love to teach people the facts and principles of the Word of God. Now, there are other men who teach the Word of God, and they all teach in a different way. For example, someone whose teaching comes across as very compassionate and merciful, probably has the gift of mercy blended in with their teaching gift.

We all are as unique as *"the manifold grace of God"* (1 Pet. 4:10b). Do you know what that means? The word *"manifold"* literally means "multi-colored." In other words, God has put a rainbow of gifts in every Christian, creating a variety of different shades.

c. **The Gifts Channeled**

With the unique spiritual gift that every Christian is given, we simply become channels through which the Spirit of God ministers to the body of Christ. And it's so marvelous to be used by God, isn't it? I've had people say to me, "John, when you teach the Word of God, I get a lot out of it and it comes alive to me. But when I talk to you in person, you're just an average guy. And you're not very profound." Well, that's right. Do you know why? Because when I'm not exercising my gift, I'm doing what I do on a human level, with all of my limitations. But as soon as I begin to minister my gift, there's a power that comes from the Spirit of God that makes things happen that can't happen when I'm dependent on my own intellect. That's exciting! Sometimes when I get up to preach, I'm anxious to hear what I'm going to say. The Spirit blends things in my mind and causes me to discover truths that I'd never seen before . . . while I'm preaching! Sometimes I think to myself, "That's a tremendous truth. Why didn't I ever see it before?"

In fact, all my books are written from the tapes of my sermons. Do you know why? Because the dynamic of God's ministry in my life is through my preaching. If I just took out a piece of paper, sat down, and began to write, nothing would ever get published. That's not where God has gifted me.

Spiritual gifts are very important. We need to be exercising them if fellowship is ever going to really take place. You say, "If that's the case, I'd better hurry up and find out what my gift is. I'll go get a computer survey and get analyzed." No, you don't need to do that. It really doesn't matter if you don't know the exact makeup of your gift. All that matters is that you be filled with the Spirit. Because if the Spirit's flowing through your life, all you have to do is step back and see what it is that you do in serving the body of Christ. Also, you'll notice that if you try to get a person to clearly define their gift, they'll find it difficult to do, because it's a beautiful blending together that resists absolute categorization. Every spiritual gift is unique, because of the uniqueness of every individual.

So, I believe God ministers in the area of fellowship through our gifts. There's another important category to look at as we consider how our fellowship becomes practical. This second category is what I call . . .

B. Mutual Ministry

1. THE EXHORTATIONS

When I say mutual ministry, I'm referring to all the "one anothers" of the New Testament. Fellowship fleshes out when we begin to practice the "one anothers." For example, we are to love one another (1 Pet. 1:22), pray for one another (Js. 5:16), edify one another (Rom. 14:19), rebuke (or reprove) one another (1 Tim. 5:20), exhort one another (Heb. 3:13), confess our sins to one another (Js. 5:16), forgive one another (Col. 3:13), bear one another's burdens (Gal. 6:2), restore one another (Gal. 6:1), comfort one another (1 Thess. 4:18), teach one another (Col. 3:16), serve one another (Gal. 5:13), be kind to one another (Eph. 4:32), submit to one another (Eph. 5:21), be hospitable to one another (1 Pet. 4:9), and minister to one another (1 Pet. 4:10). All of those "one anothers" are a part of our mutual ministry. Mutual ministry says, "I'm for you, and you're for me." That's right. Did you know that my spiritual gift is not for myself? I'm not supposed to go into a corner and teach myself. My gift isn't for me, it's for you. And if I don't minister my gift, who loses out? You do. The same is true with all the "one anothers."

When Scripture says that you're to grow spiritually, it emphasizes that the way to grow is to start giving yourself away. But that's so opposite from our self-centered society, isn't it? Our society's favorite words are me, me, me, me. Their favorite mottoes are, "Do your own thing" and "Grab all the gusto you can get." Their view of life says, "Fulfill your own needs," "Don't let anybody take your square inch of this turf," "You're the guy that matters, so do what you want and don't let anybody try and stop you." Well, that isn't the way it is in the New Testament, is it? The whole of the New Testament tells us to lose ourselves in the needs of others. That's what the "one anothers" are all about.

2. THE EXERCISE

Mutual ministry really begins to happen when we begin to minister our spiritual gift. You say, "You don't need me." Yes we do! You're a spiritual snowflake that can't be replaced. If you're not functioning, the body has to compensate somewhere else, and will be forced to limp. Why? Because there's nobody like you. You have to practice the "one anothers" and lose yourself in the needs of the body.

When people come in for counseling complaining about all their problems, I usually like to say to them, "Who are you helping? Who are you pouring your life into?" Do you know why I say that? Because people who get deeply involved in their problems will only find their way out as they begin to look away from themselves and to lose themselves in somebody else's problems and needs.

3. THE EMPHASIS

Emphasizing the "one anothers" is absolutely critical to fellowship. The church will begin to function when these things happen. I believe the leadership of the church has to generate this by teaching their congregations about spiritual gifts and how they are to function in the energy of the Spirit. We also need to teach people the one-another ministries. That's where accountability comes in. If I'm accountable to minister to you, and you're accountable to minister to me, we're going to rub against each other, and we're both going to grow.

Years ago when I played football, I had to lift weights to keep in shape. I never would have been able to do it, though, if I hadn't had somebody to do it with me—to stand across from me and get in a contest. I don't lift weights anymore, but I do ride a stationary exercise bike. I go about twelve miles a day and work up a sweat. It's great, but it's hard to stay on a consistent schedule. Fortunately, I have a friend who bought the same kind of bike at the same time I bought mine. And every time he sees me he says, "Well, how many miles do you have on your bike?" If his mileage is higher than mine, I go home and huff and puff until I'm right with him. I need that accountability. Spiritually, we all need a sense of accountability as we mutually minister, encourage, and exhort one another. That's how we put the flesh on our fellowship.

QUESTION #5: *John, how do you get a church to actually live out the elements of fellowship?*

Well, that's what I've decided to devote my life to doing—to try and get the church to work out its fellowship. As simply as possible, let me show you how to help those to whom you are ministering, to understand how to fellowship—whether it be a church, a Bible study group, or a Sunday school class. I'm going to use the metaphor of a body, and divide it into four elements. The first element I want to talk about is . . .

A. The Skeleton: *Foundational Truths*

A body has to have a skeleton in it, right? It has to have something to frame it—something that's foundational. What, then, are the primary truths we should communicate that make up the skeletal framework? First of all, I believe a church has to have . . .

1. A HIGH VIEW OF GOD

   a. ***The Compelling Character***

   Somehow you have to communicate the exalted character of God to people. You see, if I don't believe God is important, then I won't think His Word is important either. If I don't believe in the absolute majesty and authority of God, then I'm not going to be bound to do what He says, am I? The entire Bible affirms the character of God, and so must we. Why? Because people won't respond to the commands of the Bible until they know God to be the God that He is. A healthy fear of God makes people more reluctant to sin, doesn't it? Once they know that God sees them sin, and once they know that God has the right to chasten them for their sin, and once they know that He's a holy God on His holy throne, they're more reluctant to sin.

   Now that's not the only reason we don't sin. Primarily, we shouldn't sin because we love Him. But the backside of love is that we know we're in trouble if we don't obey. Weren't you that way with your parents when you were growing up? You obeyed your parents because you didn't want them to spank you, right? But at the same time, you loved them and wanted to please them. You needed both of those motivations to compel you to obey. So I believe that if we're to see fellowship be what it ought to be in the church, we must convey to people that God is on His throne, and that He is holy, majestic, and awesome.

★ *The Agreement of the Trinity on Our Unity*

Did you know that God wants unity in His church? It's not optional, it's a nonnegotiable issue. This is what God wants. And you can't ignore the statements of Jesus in John 17 when He prayed that we would be one (vv. 11, 21-23). Do you think that Jesus prayed in the will of the Father? Sure He did. Our unity, then, is the Father's will and Jesus' will. What about the Spirit? Well, it's the Spirit who creates our unity in the bond of peace (Eph. 4:3). Unity in the church is certainly the will of God!

So, if we don't have the right kind of fellowship, it may be because we don't understand who our God is, which would result in the lack of a healthy fear.

- b. **The Contrasting Concept**
    1) *The Biblical Reverence of God*

        If you go back into the Old Testament, you'll find out that God basically scared people. For example, when God came down to Mount Sinai to give Moses the law, the people were terrified. First of all, Moses told them not to touch the mountain or they would be killed. Then there was thunder and lightning and earthquakes and fire and smoke . . . all because God came down to the mount (Ex. 19:12-13, 16-18). We sometimes think of God as a benign old man in a rocking chair, but the Old Testament viewed God as a fearsome God. Sometimes people sinned and died on the spot, didn't they? Even in the New Testament, when Ananias and Sapphira lied to the Holy Spirit, they fell dead in front of the whole church (Ac. 5:1-11). Why? Because God was conveying to them that He is a God who is not to be trifled with.

    2) *The Contemporary Reduction of God*

        Contemporary Christianity doesn't take God very seriously. We've reduced God and made Him like men. Somebody once said, "God created us in His image, so now we've returned the favor." We tend to pull God down to our level, don't we? Unfortunately, we've lost the ability to respond to the awesomeness of God because we've reduced Him to Somebody that we can sort of toy with.

So, I think it's foundational to convey to people the awesomeness of God, and the fact that He deserves to be reverenced. We're not just to fear Him, we're to reverence Him as well. He is worthy of our obedience and our praise.

A second foundational truth that I think is important to convey to people is . . .

2. THE ABSOLUTE PRIORITY OF SCRIPTURE

    It's amazing to me how many Christian people don't understand how authoritative the Bible really is. It's almost as if they can take it or leave it. How many people have you heard say, "Well, that may be in the Bible, but we're not going to get into that, are we?" or "I know the Bible says I shouldn't do this, but the Lord will forgive me"? You hear that all the time, don't you? Christians who don't take God seriously, tend not to take His Scripture seriously, either.

What I'm saying is this: You can't walk into a church and say, "All right, everybody, we're all going to have fellowship now. Let's start. Okay, everybody fellowship. Go out there and minister your gifts, love everybody, and start doing all the one anothers." You can't do that before you have the framework. In the first place, they won't understand how important it is to take God seriously, and secondly they won't understand how important it is to obey His Word.

So the kind of church that's going to know real fellowship is one that has a high view of God and a high view of the authority of Scripture. I really believe that as a pastor, my primary role is to bring people under the umbrella of the authority of the Word of God. Because once they understand that the Word of God is authoritative, I can introduce any principle and they're bound by their conscience to do it. Somebody once said to me, "When you preached that sermon about the biblical role of women in our contemporary society, did all your women revolt?" I said, "No, they didn't revolt at all, because they've already made a conscious commitment to the authority of the Word of God. So when I introduce anything out of the Word of God, they're bound by the commitment that they've made to follow it. And it doesn't offend them—they want to do that." They're like Paul, who said, *"For I delight in the law of God . . ."* (Rom. 7:22).

Another skeletal truth that I think is part of the framework of a church is . . .

3. DOCTRINAL CLARITY

I don't think a church is going to be able to see its fellowship take form until they've been taught clearly what fellowship is. Too many Christians live in a doctrinal fog. They don't know what they believe about a lot of things. They can sing, "Jesus loves me this I know, for the Bible tells me so." But beyond that, they really don't have a lot of information to give. When it comes to knowing what the Bible teaches about the issues of life, they don't have a clue. I believe that it's essential for these people to be taught the truths of the Word of God, so that they're not in a fog when it comes to knowing biblical truth.

Another foundational truth that must be communicated to the church is . . .

4. PERSONAL HOLINESS

You can't create a legitimate fellowship out of lives that are plagued with sin. It can't be done! You can't take a group of people who are living in sin and say, "All right now, we're going to have a new fellowship program. All you disobedient Christians, all you unholy saints, get in there and really fellowship it up." If you did that, you'd have a terrible mess. You'd just have chaos under a different name. You can't do that. There has to be a purity of life if the fellowship is to be created by the power of the Spirit of God.

All right, that makes up the skeleton. The second thing a body needs is . . .

B. The Internal Systems: *Right Spiritual Attitudes*

Your internal systems are what makes you function. Now, to have proper fellowship in the church, we have to communicate to people that there are some internal systems. What are they? I believe that they are right spiritual attitudes. So the goal of any ministry is to convey to people that they must have right spiritual attitudes. First the framework must be set, then we have to see right attitudes flowing through the body. What are those right attitudes? Let me give you some suggestions:

1. COMMITMENT

    Commitment to the Lordship of Christ is a good one to start with. Christians must be committed to that. They're not to be halfhearted, they're to serve the Lord with their whole heart—delighting in the law of God and committed to a pure life.

    a. *The Illustration of Commitment*

        Paul illustrates real commitment in Ephesians 6:14, where he says, *"Stand, therefore, having your loins girded about with truth . . . ."* Have you ever wondered what that meant? Well, a Roman soldier basically wore a dress, which they called a tunic. It had two holes for the arms, and a hole for the head. When they put it on, it just hung down like a skirt. They would never go into battle, however, with their tunic flapping in the breeze. In hand-to-hand combat, if somebody pulled it over their head, they'd be defenseless. So to prevent that kind of disaster, they took a belt, wrapped it around their waist, tied it tightly, and then took the corners of their tunic and pulled it up through the belt. It was then cinched up real tight so that it would stay out of their way in hand-to-hand combat. They didn't want anything to encumber or distract or interrupt them as they were fighting for their existence. What Paul is saying is this: "Look, the Christian life is a war. So you'd better cinch up your belt and get dressed for battle." He's talking about commitment. We're not just lollygagging through the park picking flowers; this is war! There has to be a sense of commitment.

b. **The Issue of Commitment**

If you really analyzed it, most Christians who don't succeed, don't succeed because they're not committed. They're saved, and they get a few blessings here and there. But they're content with mediocrity. There are a few, though, that are committed. They keep pursuing excellence in their Christian walk. Paul put it this way: He said, *"Not as though I had already attained, either were already perfect . . . . I press toward the mark . . ."* (Phil. 3:12a, 14a). He also said, *"Know ye not that they who run in a race run all, but one receiveth the prize? So run, that ye may obtain. . . . I, therefore, so run, not as uncertainly; so fight I, not as one that beateth the air* [lit. 'shadowboxes']*"* (1 Cor. 9:24, 26). Now, that's the way to approach the Christian life.

So, one of the things you need to generate in a church fellowship is an attitude of commitment. When you get committed people going, you've got something exciting. To be real honest with you, as a pastor, the toughest thing to deal with in the church is the mass of uncommitted people. They come to church with a thimble, fill it up during the message, and then spill it on the steps going out. They don't go anywhere in their Christian life. They don't grow, nothing happens, and they never really know the fullness of the power of God. Instead, they make the church drag them along as baggage as it moves out in the world.

Let me give you a second internal attitude:

2. HUMILITY

Humility is an important internal attitude. Do you think that real fellowship can exist without humility? No, because I'm not going to give myself up for you unless I have a right view of myself. Humility is essential, but everything in the world says "pride": wear this kind of clothing, drive this kind of car, live in this kind of house, smell like this, do your hair like this, go to this school, work for this company, and so on. Everything is based on pride. "Come to my house, and see my display of the things that I have bought with the large sums of money my company gives me because I'm so valuable." It's all pride—the very antithesis of humility. We live in a world where pride is an issue. But in the church, humility is the only issue. So, we need to convey to people the internal attitude of humility. Another one is . . .

3. LOVE

Love rises out of humility, doesn't it? I can't love you unless I can care more about you than I care about myself. Because if I care more about me than you, all I'll want to do is get you to love me. But if I care more about you than I do myself, then I can love you. So, we need to teach people to love. Further, we have to teach people about . . .

4. UNITY
5. SERVICE
6. ACCOUNTABILITY
7. FLEXIBILITY
8. SELF-DISCIPLINE
9. FRUITFULNESS

There are many, many internal attitudes that need to be conveyed. After we get through the skeleton and the internal systems, we get to . . .

C. The Muscles: *Functions*

Now that we have the right framework, and the right stuff flowing through it, we need muscles to move it. What are the functions that we need to be actively involved in? Let me just mention some to you:

1. EVANGELISM
2. PREACHING/TEACHING
3. PRAYER
4. DISCIPLINE
5. SHEPHERDING
6. LEADERSHIP DEVELOPMENT
7. MINISTRY TRAINING
8. FAMILY MINISTRIES
9. GIVING

So, for real fellowship to occur, the church has to have a skeleton (foundational truths), internal systems (spiritual attitudes), muscles (functions/ministry), and finally, we must have . . .

D. The Flesh: *Methods*

The flesh is just the form the programs take on—which is really not an issue. If you give me a group of people who have everything else going on, you could put any kind of form on them and they'd do it, right? But people think they can just walk in and say, "Let's get the form of fellowship." What they wind up doing is dragging out a bunch of flesh that won't stand or function, because it doesn't have all that it needs internally.

So, if the church is to know real fellowship, it has to flow through this whole understanding. Rome wasn't built in a day, and you can't build the fellowship in a day, either. The other day, I read that the average pastor stays in a church a little over two years. That's not very long. And the average youth pastor stays only eighteen months. You can't even get number one on the skeleton going, in that amount of time, can you? It takes time and effort to build the things that are going to result in genuine fellowship. But when it comes, John tells us that our joy will be full (1 Jn. 1:4). Is there anything as sweet as the complete joy of fellowship? We have something going that the world doesn't know anything about—the wonderful communion of God's redeemed people. I can go to a foreign country, and be among people I've never met in my life. And if I find people who love the Lord Jesus Christ, fellowship is going on in five minutes as brothers and sisters in Christ. We all have the common, eternal life. It's amazing, though, that we can have such great fellowship with somebody we've never met before in a foreign country, but we have such a tough time fellowshiping with the guy that sits down the row from us in church who does something that irritates us. And we see him every week. Well, we have to get on with the business of fellowship!

Focusing on the Facts

1. What *isn't* our fellowship based on? What *is* the basis of our fellowship? (see p. 44)
2. What is the literal meaning of the word *fellowship*? (see p. 44)
3. Christians are joined as partners to the _____ and to _____ _____. (see p. 45)
4. Why aren't we to limit our fellowship within the boundaries of our own local assembly? (see p. 45)
5. How does our fellowship affect our testimony to the world? (see p. 45)
6. What New Testament passage clearly shows the characteristics of a fellowshiping church? What are those characteristics? (see p. 46)
7. Fellowship has to include what four areas of sharing? (see pp. 46-47)

8. Acts 2:44 says that the church *"had all things common."* What does that mean? (see p. 48)

9. What was dynamic about the first church? What were the effects of their testimony? (see p. 49)

10. The _____ _____ is the symbol of our fellowship. (see p. 49)

11. With whom does the Lord's Table celebrate our unity? (see p. 49)

12. How does the Lord's Table eliminate all the distinctions between Christians? Why is this important? (see pp. 50-51)

13. Why is the regular celebration of the Lord's Table essential in guarding against the destruction of fellowship? (see p. 51)

14. What were the effects of sin on the Corinthian assembly? (see p. 51)

15. How does 1 Peter 4:10 support the point that Christians have only one spiritual gift? (see p. 52)

16. What is the definition of a spiritual gift? (see p. 52)

17. A variety of spiritual gifts are listed in 1 Corinthians 12 and in Romans 12. Is 1 Peter 4:10 saying that every Christian receives one of these specific gifts? Explain. (see pp. 52-53)

18. Explain why people who have the gift of teaching, for example, all teach with different styles and emphases. (see p. 53)

19. What is meant by the comment that we are all spiritual snowflakes, in terms of our spiritual gifts? (see p. 53)

20. Is it optional for Christians to be exercising their spiritual gift? Explain. (see p. 54)

21. Is it essential to be able to identify your spiritual gift before you exercise it? Why or why not? (see p. 54)

22. Why might it be difficult for someone to actually define their gift? (see p. 54)

23. Name five of the "one anothers" in the New Testament. Why are the "one anothers" important to fellowship? Do we have to obey all of them, or can we choose the ones that we are most gifted in? (see p. 55)

24. What is good counsel to give to someone who is overwhelmed with all of their problems? (see p. 56)

25. What role does accountability play in fellowship? (see p. 56)

26. In describing the church as a body, it can be broken down to four essential parts. What are they, and what does each one represent? (see pp. 57-63)

27. What are the four foundational truths that must be communicated and emphasized if a church is to have real fellowship? (see pp. 57-60)

28. What effect does a high view of God have upon a person's sinful habits? Why? (see p. 57)

29. How is our contemporary view of God different from that of the people in Exodus 19:16? Which view is more conducive to proper fellowship? Why? (see p. 58)

30. Why is it essential to affirm the absolute priority of Scripture before true fellowship can occur? (see pp. 58-59)

31. What relationship does an understanding of fellowship have to the actual practice of fellowship? (see p. 59)

32. Can legitimate fellowship take place with believers who are being disobedient to God's Word? Explain. (see p. 60)

33. What happens when someone tries to stimulate fellowship, simply with someone else's program? (see p. 60)

34. The metaphor of the internal systems of the body signifies what important element of church fellowship? (see p. 60)

35. What is Paul illustrating when he refers to a soldier girding up his loins? (see pp. 60-61)

36. How does a personal attitude of commitment affect the corporate fellowship of the church? Why? (see p. 61)

37. Why is humility essential to fellowship? (see p. 61)

38. Once a church has the skeleton and the internal systems, what is the next element of the body that needs to be established? What does this represent? (see p. 62)

39. What functions must a church be actively involved in to see real fellowship occur? (see p. 62)

40. The fourth element of the body metaphor is the flesh. What does this represent? How does this rank with the other three elements in terms of importance? Why? (see p. 63)

Pondering the Principles
(For Group Discussion)

1. What are some of the artificial barriers to fellowship? How do these barriers arise? Discuss any artificial barriers to fellowship that you personally might have, and any that your church might have. What steps can you take to remove these barriers?

2. Who does John 13:35 apply to? What are the consequences if this is limited only to believers within individual churches? Does this verse support an ecumenical movement? Explain your answer.

3. How does your church measure up to each of the characteristics of the church described in Acts 2:42-47? What are you currently doing to help your church follow that first church's pattern? What else could you do?

4. What perspective must we have if we are to emulate the sharing that took place in Acts 2:44-45? Is this kind of sharing taking place in churches today? Is it taking place in your church? Is it taking place in your own life? What are some practical steps that you can take to develop a more caring attitude to those who have needs?

5. What is the purpose in celebrating the Lord's Table? Why is this essential to true fellowship? Do you consider it a priority in your own life? Why is it a good idea to celebrate the Lord's Table on a regular basis?

6. What is the definition of a spiritual gift? What is its purpose? Do you have any comments on the idea that every Christian has one unique spiritual gift, which has been combined from a variety of spiritual gifts? Do you know the categories that the Spirit has gifted you in? Are you involved in ministering your unique gift? If you aren't exercising your spiritual gift, what effect does it have on the body of Christ?

7. Look over the "one anothers" on page 55, and discuss how each one is important to fellowship. Which ones do you find yourself most often involved in? Which ones do you have difficulty with? Commit yourself to become accountable on a weekly basis to another Christian in the areas of exercising your spiritual gift and practicing the "one anothers."

8. What are the four foundational truths that make up the skeletal framework for the body of Christ? Consider each one separately, and discuss how it specifically affects fellowship.

9. On a scale of one to ten, how would you rate the overall commitment level of the people in your church? How would you rate your own commitment level? What steps can you take to increase your personal commitment level? What steps can the leaders of your church take to increase the commitment level of the congregation?

10. It takes time and effort to build the things that are going to result in genuine fellowship. How much time each week are you willing to devote to building genuine fellowship within your own church? What specific effort are you going to make?

Selected Scriptures Tape GC 2033

HOW TO WITNESS

Introduction

So far in this series, we've talked about some very important topics relating to the Christian life. We've talked about prayer, the study of the Word of God, and fellowship—all of which operate within the family of God. There's one more topic, however, that we need to talk about: witnessing to those who are outside the family of God. Now indirectly, if everything is right in all those other areas, we're going to have an impact on people outside the family of God. But we need to talk a little bit about the direct approach of communicating the saving gospel of Jesus Christ to others.

In John 15:26, Jesus said, *"But when the Comforter is come, whom I will send unto you from the Father, even the Spirit of truth, who proceedeth from the Father, He shall testify of Me."* Now the first thing we learn from that verse is that the Holy Spirit is in the business of witnessing. The Holy Spirit has come to testify of the truth concerning Christ. Continuing on in verse 27, Jesus said to His disciples, *"And ye also shall bear witness, because ye have been with Me from the beginning."* The Holy Spirit, then, was sent into the world, and into our hearts, to bear witness of Christ. He, therefore, bears witness through us. And we who have been with Christ, are firsthand witnesses to who He is and what He can do in a life. The ministry of witnessing is committed to us. Acts 1:8 says, *"But ye shall receive power, after the Holy Spirit is come upon you; and ye shall be witnesses . . . ."* We're all called, then, to communicate the saving gospel of Jesus Christ.

QUESTION #1: *John, does a person have to be specially trained to witness?*

 It's good to have some training, but anyone who knows Jesus Christ can do it. That's the only condition.

 A. The Clarification of Witnessing

  Years ago, I was an assistant pastor at the church where my father was serving as pastor. One day, the secretary came running in through the church door and said, "There is a fight in the parking lot!" It was a boring day, so I decided to go out and watch it. Just fifty feet from where I came out the door, there was a man lying in the dirt, with two men kicking him and pummeling his body. At that point, I realized that this was very serious, so I said, "Hey, you guys, break it up!" When they didn't respond, I thought, "Well, maybe they didn't hear me," so I yelled a little louder: "Break it up!" Still, they didn't respond. As I approached them, I heard one of the men say, "Kill him . . . kill him!" At that point, I realized that I was watching an attempted murder—not an ordinary fight. By the time I got to the scene, the guy was such a bloody mess, I couldn't even distinguish his face. One of the attackers—a six-foot-five, two-hundred-and-fifty-pound professional dockworker who played rugby—turned toward me and said, "What do you want?" I was paralyzed for a moment because of this man's size, but I finally said, "You better break it up and leave this guy alone!" When he pulled back his fist, my instinctive reaction was to back up. I backed up, but both he and his accomplice started coming after me. I kept backing up, drawing them away from their victim, until I arrived at the church door. Once I stepped through the door, I thought to myself, "They're not going to come into the church. So I'll go get somebody to call the police." Was I ever wrong! They came right in! My dad, who had been studying all this time, came out of his office. When he said, "What's going on here?" the big guy took a swing at him. At that point, I yelled, "Someone call the police!" Suddenly they panicked, ran back outside, picked up their senseless victim, smashed his head against a wall, dropped him behind a bush, and ran for a getaway car. Fortunately, I was able to write down the license number and give it to the police when they arrived. The man who had been beaten up was still alive, but because he was so scared of these men, he wouldn't press charges against them. In fact, after they were caught, he wouldn't even testify against them. So, the court called me in as a witness.

As long as I live, I'll never forget what happened when I went to court. When I got up to testify, they said, "Do you swear to tell the truth, the whole truth, and nothing but the truth?" After I replied, "I do," the attorney walked up to me and said, "Reverend MacArthur, you tell us what you saw, what you heard, and what you felt." That is exactly what he asked me. And on those terms, I instantly became a witness. What I saw, what I heard, and what I felt made me a viable witness, because I was there.

B. The Conditions of Witnessing

Ever since that event, when the subject of witnessing comes up, I always think of what John said in 1 John 1: *"That . . . which we have heard, which we have seen with our eyes, which we have looked upon, and our hands have handled, of the Word of life . . . declare we unto you . . ."* (vv. 1, 3b).

1. THE PREREQUISITES

What is a witness? Somebody who has seen, heard, and felt the power of Jesus Christ. So the answer to the question, "Who can be a witness?" is this: Anybody who has been with Christ is a viable witness. John 15:27 says, *"And ye also shall bear witness, because ye have been with Me from the beginning."* Once you know Jesus Christ, and you have seen Him, heard Him, and touched Him in your life, you become one who can speak concerning Him. You may not know all the doctrines of the Bible, and you may not know every in and out of theology, and you may not know all the little systems, gimmicks, methods, and angles. But if you have walked with Jesus Christ, you have something to say. You are a firsthand, living testimony to the power of Jesus Christ—which is far more important than knowing a formula.

2. THE POWER

I knew a preacher who got up in front of his church one day, and said, "I just want you to know, that even though I've been the pastor of this church for ten years, today I came to know Jesus Christ as my Savior." Only at that point, for the first time in his life, did he become a witness to the power of Jesus Christ. Before that, he knew all the facts and the methods, but he didn't know Christ or the personal power that comes in the energy of the Spirit of God.

So, who can be a witness? Anyone who is a Christian—anyone who knows Jesus Christ.

C. **The Command to Witness**

We're mandated to witness! Jesus said to the disciples, *"Go ye into all the world, and preach the gospel to every creature"* (Mk. 16:15). All of us are mandated to go out and communicate the Christ that we have seen, heard, and felt. It's obviously a terrible thing to defer from that. To not tell the world what we know of Jesus Christ is to withhold from them the greatest truth they'll ever hear. Every one of us that is a Christian, then, is a witness.

D. **The Conduct of Witnessing**

Did you know that if people know you're a Christian, you're a witness even if you don't say anything? You may not be a very good one, but you're still a witness nonetheless. Why? Because people read the meaning of Christ in your life by the life that you live. And if you don't say anything about Christ to them, they'll perceive that He isn't that valuable or that meaningful to you. If you've hidden your Christianity for years, and someone who has known you for a long time finds out that you're a Christian, he'll conclude that it isn't very important to you, or that it's a secret society only for the initiated. Jesus said, *"And ye are witnesses of these things"* (Lk. 24:48). We are witnesses. He doesn't ask us if we'd like to be witnesses, He simply says, "You are witnesses; just be sure you're effective ones." And only a Christian can be an effective witness.

Let me add one thing: The gospel is so powerful that even in the mouth of that preacher I mentioned who wasn't a Christian, the gospel itself could transcend his lack of experience and affect people's lives. After all, God was able to use Balaam's ass, right? The gospel is so powerful, that it can transcend the vehicle. But in order to be a true and effective witness, you have to know Jesus Christ. That's really all there is to it . . . at least to start.

QUESTION #2: *John, I've heard a variety of different definitions of witnessing, but what is witnessing all about?*

First of all, witnessing is defined as "a person communicating testimony about something they have experienced." In a legal trial, the courts don't want secondhand witnesses, do they? No! They want eyewitnesses. They want to hear testimony from someone who was actually there. Someone with information passed down through several sources is not a valid witness.

Let me give you a perspective that will clarify this concept:

A. The Representation of Witnessing

Christ is on trial before the world, isn't He? The world, as the jury, is trying to make a decision about Jesus Christ. The Holy Spirit, as the lawyer for the defense, has taken up Christ's case in the world. His task is to convince the world that Christ is who He says He is. To present His case, the Holy Spirit calls witnesses into the courtroom. Well, we are those witnesses! We are witnesses for the defense of Jesus Christ before the watching world. That's a serious role, isn't it?

If you, for example, were called into the Supreme Court of the United States of America, and somebody asked you to defend Jesus Christ, would you do it if He was actually on trial there? Of course you would! I've often thought, "If I had been there when He was being tried before Caiaphas, or before Annas, I would have said some things in His defense. I wouldn't let those guys get away with false judgments on Christ. He deserved better than that!"

Well, our society is making a judgment on Christ. The world that we live in is a courtroom. And the Spirit of God, as the lawyer for the defense, calls us as witnesses to give our testimony. We must realize, if we're to properly understand witnessing, that there are people who are going to make their conclusions about Jesus Christ based upon our testimony. So, as we begin to understand witnessing, we have to recognize that the Holy Spirit is calling us to be witnesses for Christ.

B. The Reaction to Witnessing

Let me ask you a question: What is it that makes a person willing to be a witness? I believe that it's the element of sacrifice. There is a price to pay when you name the name of Jesus Christ. You can't confront a godless, Christless world and not expect to get some reaction.

A few years ago, I had the opportunity to speak in an open forum on the campus of a large local university. They had asked me to speak on the topic: "Christianity and Culture." Well, everything I know about Christianity's relationship to culture, can be exhausted in about ten minutes. So I decided that since the predominant number of the several thousand students that had gathered didn't know Jesus Christ, I would spend the rest of the sixty minutes allotted to me to speak on the deity of Jesus Christ and how to know God through Him. Well, for forty minutes I proclaimed the deity of Christ and salvation through Him . . . and you could have heard a pin drop. The Spirit of God was in obvious control.

There are times when preaching is very difficult. Sometimes I feel like I'm pushing against a lot of resistance. But there are other times when I preach, that I feel like I'm flying. On this particular day, I was soaring. I felt the power of God as He was using me to reach these students for Christ. When I was finished speaking, a young man walked up to me and said, "I need to know Jesus Christ," and the Lord gave me the privilege of leading him to Christ. Another young man, who I had the privilege of seeing in my office a few days later, came to Christ and eventually went to seminary.

God really touched some lives that day, but not without having other effects as well: Christian lecturers were banned from the campus; the free speech platform was closed down; the Christian book table was removed from the campus; and the next time I spoke at a nearby college, the group of students that had protested the last time I spoke, came over from their campus, surrounded the podium where I was speaking, and shouted the whole time. They threatened to bomb the church, and they called our home in the middle of the night with obscene phone calls—threatening my wife and family.

Well, my first reaction was, "I have to quit doing this! It's creating problems." But my second reaction was, "I think I made a wave—a small dent in the kingdom of darkness." I also began to understand a little more of what Peter was saying in 1 Peter 4:14 when he said, *"If ye be reproached for the name of Christ, happy are ye; for the Spirit of glory and of God resteth upon you . . . ."* And there was a tremendous sense of identification, as I was experiencing just a small taste of the kind of persecution the early Christians went through.

So, when you approach the responsibility of standing before the world to testify for the sake of Jesus Christ, you have to realize that this hostile world is going to react when the gospel is truly preached.

C. The Responsibility in Witnessing

If your witnessing consists of nothing more than a discussion of God's love and all the benefits of the Christian life, and you never confront people with their sin and the fact that they live in violation of God's law, they probably will not react negatively. But they haven't been given the true gospel, either, have they? As witnesses, we have to confront the truth of sin and righteousness, and proclaim the truth about Jesus Christ. When you do that, however, there's a sacrifice to be made.

Are you going to keep your mouth closed and not make any sacrifice? Is your own personal reputation worth more to you than testifying of Christ? Or are you willing to say, "Hey, I don't really care what happens to me. I'm expendable!"? Paul, in talking about *"holding forth the word of life,"* says, *"Yea, and if I be offered upon the sacrifice and service of your faith, I joy, and rejoice with you all"* (Phil. 2:16a, 17). In other words, "If I die getting you saved . . . sweet death." That's the kind of sacrifice we're talking about.

★ *John Paton: Willing to Pay the Price*

> John Paton went to the New Hebrides Islands to be a missionary. Now, that was a tough assignment, because these islands were inhabited by cannibals. I would have said, "Lord, don't send me there. They'll eat me, and You'll waste a good one. After all, I graduated from seminary. Why don't You send someone who dropped out? They'll eat him, and who will know? Maybe he would have never made it anyway. But don't send me!" Well, Paton didn't argue with God's call. When he and his wife arrived at the islands, they were dropped off so that they had to row to shore. There they built a little lean-to.
>
> Now, how do you reach natives like that? What would you do? You can't put up a sign in the sand that says, "VBS starts Saturday, bring your children." Well, they prayed a lot. Night after night they stayed in that little lean-to and prayed

> for a way to reach those cannibals with the gospel of Christ. It's interesting to note that when one of the chiefs came to know Jesus Christ years later, he asked Paton who the soldiers were that ringed his little lean-to every night with the shining armor. God apparently protected him with His holy angels.
>
> After he had been there a couple of months, his wife gave birth to a baby. Unfortunately, the baby died; and a few days later, his wife died. Paton buried their bodies, but he had to sleep on their graves to keep the natives from digging them up and eating them. All alone, and seemingly at the end of his rope, he had to make a decision: "Do I stay, or do I go?"
>
> Well, John Paton stayed . . . for thirty-five years! And at the end of those thirty-five years he was able to say, "I do not know of one single native on these islands who has not made at least a profession of faith in Jesus Christ. When I first came, I heard the cry of cannibals; but as I leave, I hear the ringing of church bells." Isn't that incredible? But that's what can happen if you're willing to make a sacrifice. Not everybody will be a John Paton, but everybody can do what God's called them to do if they're willing to pay the price.

So, to be a testimony in the world, you have to realize that there's a price to pay. If you're a Christian who is sold out to Christ, you are willing to pay that price—not just once . . . but from now on. That battle of whether you're willing to speak for Christ will always be there.

QUESTION #3: *John, with all the sacrifice and commitment involved in witnessing, and the frustration that occurs when people don't respond to the gospel, why can't we just pursue God and read His Word? After all, doesn't God sovereignly bring men to Himself anyway?*

In other words, there's so much heartache and disappointment involved in witnessing, wouldn't it be better to just retreat and commune with God, and let Him sovereignly take care of the saving? Well, it's not for us to figure out those kind of things. We can't say, "God, You have a good plan, but I think I have a better one. I'd like to suggest it to You." To think thoughts like that is to assume that our minds are ultimate. In other words, if we can't figure it out, it certainly can't be reasonable. However, the Bible gives us reasons to witness. For example:

A. Witnessing Is Commanded

We're supposed to witness because God tells us to. That alone is enough of a reason to witness, isn't it? Have you ever told one of your little children to do something, and you get back the standard answer, "Why?"? Now there are times when you can't explain why because they won't understand why. So you simply have to say, "Because I told you to . . . end of discussion." Well, that's the way we are. We are little children in terms of comparing ourselves with God's infinite mind. So when God tells us to witness, and we say, "Hey, I took in all the available data, and I don't understand why I should do that," He simply responds, "That's not for you to ask, just do it!" We're commanded to witness. In Matthew 28:19 Jesus said, *"Go therefore and make disciples of all the nations . . ."* (NASB). Well, that's enough for me!

Somebody once said to Charles Spurgeon, "Mr. Spurgeon, since you believe in the doctrine of election—that certain people are elect for salvation—why don't you just preach to the elect?" Spurgeon replied, "If you'll go around and pull up their shirttails so I can see if they have an *E* stamped on their back, I will." Spurgeon's point was this: Since only God knows who is elect, our responsibility is to preach to everybody. God will take care of His part. So, it's our responsibility to *"preach the gospel to every creature"* (Mk. 16:15b).

★ **Will God send someone to hell who's never heard the gospel?**

I've heard many people say, "If someone doesn't hear the gospel he's not lost, because he hasn't had an opportunity." Well, if that were true, it would be best to never give anyone the gospel. Then no one could ever reject it. But that's contrary to Christ's command, isn't it? So the fact that we're told to go preach to every creature means that even the ones who haven't heard are lost. You say, "Will God really send someone to hell, out of His presence forever, who has never heard the gospel?" Well, the Bible says that if a person lives up to the light he has, God will give him more light. And if someone hasn't heard the fullness of the gospel, it's because he hasn't yet believed the truth that has already been revealed to him (see Rom. 1:18-21). God will never send someone out of His presence forever who has not refused the truth, because God will bring the truth to the open heart.

So, our responsibility is to be obedient, and to go out and preach the gospel. Don't try to get into all kinds of rational arguments about it. We are also responsible to witness because . . .

B. Witnessing Is Not a Matter of Theological Knowledge

I think that every Christian is responsible to witness. Somebody might say, "But I'm not trained! I can't witness until I've had my training. I have to be built up so that I can answer all the arguments and all the questions." Well, we're all witnesses because we're commanded to be, and because it isn't a matter of theological knowledge. First and foremost, it's a matter of what we've seen, heard, and felt. That's where our witnessing begins. You may know very little. You may only know that Jesus saved you. But that's enough!

We have baptismal services in our church all the time, and the power of the personal testimonies is overwhelming. Nobody ever discusses deep theological issues like the doctrine of homoousion (the being of God), or discusses the difference between sublapsarianism, infralapsarianism, and a labrador retriever. No one ever gives big theological treatises in seminary language. All they do is tell what they were like before they were saved, and how God has changed them since they've been saved.

I'll never forget a guy that we baptized one night. His vocabulary wasn't very polished (which caused a few of the older saints to have a little bit of a problem), but his testimony went something like this: "I was the head of the Hell's Angels in Houston," he said. "The last time I was in a church, we rode our motorcycles down the middle aisle, threw a rope around the pastor as he was preaching his sermon, and dragged him outside and down the street." This guy even wound up in prison on a murder charge, but because it wasn't first degree, he was out. Then he made this incredible statement to the congregation: "I'm here to tell you that during the last few weeks of my time in prison I came to know Jesus Christ. And I'm here now because I want to worship Him." Now you don't have to have a whole lot of theology to give a testimony like that, do you? That's powerful! And when people hear that kind of a testimony they say, "Wow! Can Jesus Christ transform somebody like that?"

We've also had testimonies from people who have said, "For years and years I was a homosexual, but Christ has changed my life," or "For years and years I was an average good guy without fulfillment and meaning, but Christ has given me peace and joy." That's where the witnessing begins. Don't back away from that. You need to realize that we witness because we're commanded to, and because that we're fit to, if Christ has changed our life. It will become easier to answer questions and objections later on, but you still have the power of a transformed life. That is what's so very, very important.

QUESTION #4: *John, you've made it clear that we're supposed to witness, but what are the elements of effective witnessing?*

That's an important question, because some of us have tried to witness, and then walked away saying, "There must have been a better way. There must have been another approach. They tuned me out when I was only on step one!" Well, let me show you what we really need to know about witnessing:

A. The Elements of Effective Witnessing

1. THE CORPORATE TESTIMONY OF A PURE CHURCH

    Basically the corporate testimony of the church is foundational. In other words, the reputation in the community of the church that you attend, sets the foundation for whether or not anybody's going to listen to what you have to say.

    a. ***The Examples***

    1) *The Negative Effects*

        Let's say you attend a church where they are having a fight. The church is split because the pastor ran off with the secretary. And to top it off, this chaotic situation hits the newspaper, so the whole town knows about it. Now, if you were to go up to someone at school, or at work, or in your neighborhood, and start talking to him about the Lord, he might say, "You go to that church down there where the pastor just ran off with the secretary, don't you?" End of testimony, right? The corporate testimony of the church sets the foundation to make the individual witness meaningful and believable.

        One of the attorneys that attends our church came to me one Sunday and said, "I had a terrible experience this week. I invited one of my colleagues to come to church with me and he asked what church I went to. When I told him I go to Grace Community Church with John MacArthur as the pastor, he said, 'You go to that church? You've got to be kidding! I'd never go to that church. The most crooked attorney in this city goes to that church.' "

Well, I got up in the pulpit that morning and related the incident. I said, "I don't know which of you is that crooked attorney, but I wish you'd get your life cleaned up. You're making it very hard for the others to witness."

Do you understand the point? You're out in the world, and you're going to have to defend the Christianity you belong to. It's tough sometimes, isn't it? Because the media loves to play up the bad things that happen to Christian people. So, we have to live a consistent life. We have to be salt and light in the world.

2) *The Positive Effects*

Some of our effectiveness in witnessing, then, is dependent upon other people and the foundation of believability that they have laid. Have you ever witnessed to somebody who had already met so many dear, good, solid Christians that you were able to go sailing on through the gospel presentation without any resistance at all? That just shows the importance of the corporate testimony of the church, doesn't it?

b. **The Exhortations**

In John 13:35 Jesus said, *"By this shall all men know that ye are My disciples, if ye have love one to another."* That shows the purity of the church. In 1 Peter 2:12 Peter exhorts us to have our *"behavior honest among the Gentiles."* And in Paul's letters to Timothy and Titus, he told them to choose leaders in the church whose lives were blameless in the world (1 Tim. 3:2, 10; Tit. 1:6-7); because if the world can shoot down your leaders, they'll destroy your testimony.

So, in a very real sense, we're dependent on one another's testimony. What you do in your life may affect my testimony, and what I do may affect yours. When you try to share Christ with someone and they say, "I met a Christian who was such-and-such and so-and-so. I'm not interested," it reiterates the importance of the corporate witness of the church.

Now, let me talk a little bit about another element of effective witnessing. From the corporate testimony of a pure church, we move to . . .

2. THE INDIVIDUAL TESTIMONY OF A PURE LIFE

It is essential to witnessing that your life be right. The place you're going to have the most impact in your witnessing is the environment in which you live all the time. That's where you sink or swim, isn't it? You say, "Oh, it's so hard to win my family to Christ." That's right, because unless they see the virtue of Jesus Christ coming through you, day in and day out, it's going to make it tough (from the human viewpoint). Now, we know that God is the One who works in a person's life, but it's our responsibility to lay the foundation with a pure life.

First Peter 2:15 says, *"For such is the will of God that by doing right you may silence the ignorance of foolish men"* (NASB). People want to slander Christianity, but your virtuous life will shut the mouths of the critics. We all long for a Christianity that's blameless, don't we? Wouldn't you love to be demonstrating to the world the blamelessness of a Christian's life? Not perfection, but an honest, upright integrity that says, "Sure, I fail. But I go to the Lord and He helps me with those things." That's really what we want as a foundation for our witness.

3. THE PRESENTATION OF THE GOSPEL

Now, once the foundations of the corporate witness of the church and the individual witness of a pure life have been established, it's essential that you present the gospel.

   a. **Articulating One's Need**

   It's important that people hear how Christ changed your life, because most people that come to Christ come because they feel a need. People feel incomplete, lonely, depressed, and unfulfilled. They're looking for pleasure and love, but they're not finding it. They're looking for freedom from guilt because it's destroying them, but they can't throw it off. Frankly, I think that mental institutions are packed with people who have tremendous anxiety caused by guilt. People are experiencing a purposelessness and meaninglessness in life, and many are unable to rise above their own passions.

   Receptivity to the gospel, then, often starts with a felt need. So when you witness to somebody, it's good to tell them about the peace, purpose, and fulfillment you found in Jesus Christ. That's good to do initially, but it's not enough. You can't stop there. It must be taken another step:

   b. **Affirming One's Sinfulness**

   In Mark 10, the rich young ruler came to Jesus because he had a felt need. Verse 17 says that he came running up to Jesus, which tells me that this guy had some problems . . . he was hurting. Sliding in on his knees, he looks up to Jesus and says, *". . . what shall I do that I may inherit eternal life?"* That was a felt need, wasn't it? But notice that the Lord didn't say, "Just sign on the dotted line and you're in." Instead, the Lord hit him with something that was absolutely unbelievable—He told him that he had to keep all the commandments (Mt. 19:19). Do you know what the Lord was doing? He was taking him to the next step in evangelism. He was taking him beyond the acknowledgment of his need to the affirmation of his sinfulness. Jesus wanted him to realize that he was living in sin and rebellion against God.

Sometimes this is the hardest thing to tell someone. People can get all excited about finding meaning and purpose and value and fulfillment and potential, but you can't stop there. You have to go beyond that and say, "The reason you don't know those things in your life is because you're living in rebellion to the God who gives them. You must come to grips with that rebellion, and realize that you're living in violation of God's law. You're a sinner who has broken God's commandments." Then you can even describe those commandments to bring them to the point where they admit their sinfulness.

After Jesus told the rich young ruler that he had to keep the commandments to obtain eternal life, and after He listed those commandments for him, do you know what the rich young ruler said? *"All these things have I kept from my youth up. What lack I yet?"* (Mt. 19:20). It was impossible to bring that guy to conversion because he wouldn't admit that he was a sinner. He wouldn't admit that he was out of sync with God. All he was looking for was a placebo. All he wanted was temporary relief from the symptoms. He wouldn't admit that there was a deeper problem.

People must be taken to the point where they affirm the fact that they are sinful—which is sometimes very hard to do. Then they must be taken one step further. They need to be taken to the point of . . .

c. **Acknowledging Christ's Lordship**

Do you remember what Jesus told the rich young ruler? He said, *". . . go and sell what thou hast, and give to the poor . . . and come and follow Me"* (Mt. 19:21). When he heard that, the text says, *". . . he went away sorrowful; for he had great possessions"* (v. 22b). You see, he wanted to be the lord of his own life. Yes, he wanted eternal life, peace, freedom from anxiety, and all of that; but he wasn't willing to accept it if he had to admit he was a sinner. He desperately needed to preserve his own sense of self-esteem, and there was no way he was going to subject his life to the lordship of somebody else. But those are the conditions we have to bring people to.

A fourth element of effective witnessing is . . .

4. THE RECOGNITION OF THE HOLY SPIRIT'S POWER

When you witness, you need to recognize that you're dependent upon the power of the Spirit of God. You say, "Well, why is that important?" Because it keeps you from manipulating people. It's very easy, sometimes, to manipulate somebody who's emotionally agitated and in desperate need. So to be sure you don't do that, you need to recognize your dependency on the Spirit of God.

a. **His Power to Save**

Nobody has ever been saved by your cleverness, my cleverness, or anybody else's cleverness. You don't con people into being Christians. Salvation is a supernatural miracle, so we're dependent upon the power of the Spirit of God. I love that story in Acts 16 about Lydia, the liberated lady. Paul came and preached the gospel, and it says that the Lord opened her heart (v. 14). Isn't that good? The Lord is the One who opened her heart.

Somebody once said to me, "Do you get distressed when people don't respond to the gospel and receive Jesus Christ?" Well, there's a sense in which my heart is sad, but God never called me to save people—He only called me to preach the gospel to them. Saving them is His business. So I don't have a lot of anxiety about that. If I've been faithful to clearly discharge the presentation of the gospel, that's all I can do. I'm not going to manipulate people to do something on an emotional level that isn't genuine, and I'm not going to assume that I'm the one who can get people saved.

b. **His Power to Convict**

Who is it that convicts of sin, righteousness, and judgment? According to John 16:7-11, it's the Spirit. Jesus said, *"And when He* [the Spirit] *is come, He will reprove* [or 'convict'] *the world of sin, and of righteousness, and of judgment"* (v. 8).

c. **His Power to Enlighten**

In 1 Corinthians 2:9 it says, *"But as it is written, Eye hath not seen, nor ear heard, neither have entered into the heart of man, the things which God hath prepared for them that love Him."* Do you know what that's saying? Men, on their own terms, can't understand what God has for them. Unsaved men can't understand all the blessings and benefits of salvation. They can't! When it says, *". . . Eye hath not seen, nor ear heard . . . ,"* it means that it's not available objectively or empirically. It isn't out there where you can grab it. And when it says, *". . . neither have entered into the heart . . . ,"* it's saying that it's not available subjectively, or rationally. So, man can't know it outside himself, and he can't know it inside himself. You say, "Then how's he going to know it?" Verse 10 says, *"But God hath revealed them unto us by His Spirit . . . ."*

So when you're witnessing to someone, you really have to watch the Spirit of God do His work. It's such a wonderful confidence to be a part of His work and to know that the Spirit of God will use us as we're involved.

Now that brings us to *our* responsibility. We've been talking about the responsibility of the Holy Spirit; what is our responsibility? Well, let's look, now, at . . .

B. The Method of Effective Witnessing

Let's get right into talking about the actual method of witnessing. How do we go about it? Let me see if I can crystallize some of the things I've already said. First of all, I'd like to suggest that you . . .

1. SHARE YOUR PERSONAL TESTIMONY

You need to tell others how Christ came into your life, so that they don't see the salvation experience as something very bizarre and mysterious. The testimonies that people give are similar, yet diverse. For example, I've heard people say, "The other day I was driving on the freeway and I was saved," or "I was sitting in my living room when the Lord convicted me," or "I was by my bed," or "I was talking to a friend," or "I was in a restaurant," or "I happened to be in a church service." It's diverse, isn't it? We're all saved in different places, and under different circumstances. But a good place to start is with a personal testimony, because it puts Christ into a real-life situation. So when you witness to somebody, start with what Christ has done in your own life. In fact, you might even bring up your former dissatisfaction and how Christ has transformed you—if you were old enough to know that. I'll never forget the prayer of a little five-year-old boy in the prayer room. He said, "O God, save me from being a miserable sinner." Well, how miserable can you be at five?

Basically, though, you need to start with a personal testimony because that puts it into a real-life context. Then, the next step is to . . .

2. USE SCRIPTURE TO EXPLAIN YOUR CONVERSION

As you explain your conversion, make a transition to Scripture, and let the Scriptures speak for themselves. The Word of God is alive and powerful (Heb. 4:12), so you definitely want to use it in your personal testimony. For example, to show people that they're sinful, read them Romans 3:23, which says, *"For all have sinned, and come short of the glory of God."* Read them John 1:12: *"But as many as received Him, to them gave He power to become the children of God . . . ."* When you explain conversion, use the Word of God. You might even want to take them to John 3 and just go through the account of Nicodemus. Or go to Matthew 19 and talk about the rich young ruler and why he didn't become a believer. But the point is: Use Scripture. Then . . .

3. EMPHASIZE THE BROKEN LAW OF GOD

People must see themselves as sinners in need of salvation, having violated an infinitely holy God. You can't preach the good news until you tell the bad news, right? You can't preach grace unless they understand law. And they'll never understand mercy unless they understand judgment. So you have to talk about the law of God. The book of Romans, which is the essence of the gospel, begins with three chapters indicting the entire human race. Everyone is sufficiently indicted, so that *". . . every mouth may be stopped, and all the world may become guilty before God"* (3:19b). Paul shows that no one can defend themselves against their violation of the law of God. But into that comes the gospel of Jesus Christ.

So, you have to talk about the law, but then you should . . .

4. PRESENT THE GRACE OF GOD

Once you present the grace of God, you're to . . .

5. AFFIRM THE NEED FOR REPENTANCE

When Jesus came, His message was: *"Repent; for the kingdom of heaven is at hand"* (Mt. 4:17b). The prophets were constantly calling for Israel's repentance and saying, "Turn, ye; turn, ye." Once you've talked about repentance, you want to . . .

6. TALK ABOUT SUBMISSION AND OBEDIENCE TO CHRIST

Romans 10:9 says, *". . . if you confess with your mouth Jesus as Lord, and believe in your heart that God raised Him from the dead, you shall be saved"* (NASB). You have to believe the right truths, but you also have to confess His Lordship.

Now I don't believe that in order for a person to come to Christ he has to understand the full implications of His Lordship, or the full implications of what it means to turn from sin. But I do believe that there must be a willingness to submit to His Lordship. I also believe that that willingness can only be accomplished by the power of God working in that person's heart. I don't think that a normal person, apart from the work of God, is going to turn from his sin. That's part of the saving work of God. And in the same way, I don't think that a person is going to affirm Christ's Lordship, apart from the power of Christ in his life. That's part of the saving work as well. Jesus said, *"With men this is impossible, but with God all things are possible"* (Mt. 19:26b). On their own, men aren't going to turn from sin or affirm the Lordship of Christ; but God can work in the heart to accomplish that. It's necessary for salvation!

QUESTION #5: *After you've been allowed the privilege of leading someone to the Lord, what responsibilities do you have in that person's life?*

The subject of follow-up is really important, isn't it? What do you do after you've led someone to the Lord? Well, some basic elements of follow-up are found in one passage—1 Corinthians 4:14-21—as they flow out of Paul's relationship with the Corinthians. In verse 15 he says, *". . . in Christ Jesus I have begotten you through the gospel."* In other words, he says, "I led you to Christ. You're my spiritual children."

Having established that he led them to Christ, let's look, now, at what Paul does to follow them up:

A. Love Them (v. 14b)

". . . as my beloved sons . . ."

I think you need to love someone you've led to Christ, and demonstrate a genuine concern for that person. That's the key to follow-up! They need to know you love them.

1. LOVE DEFINED

    What does it mean to love somebody? Does it mean feeling emotional about them or getting spiritual goosebumps? No. John 3:16 says, *"For God so loved the world, that He gave . . . ."* First John 3:17 says that if you see a brother with a need, but you close up your compassion from him, you don't love him at all. In John 13:34, Jesus said that He wanted His disciples to love each other as He had just loved them. And how had He just loved them? By washing their dirty feet and meeting their need. Love is giving service—sacrificial service—to someone with a need.

2. LOVE DEMONSTRATED

    I believe that the best way to follow somebody up, is to demonstrate that you really do love them. This can be done by giving up some of your own time, your own priorities, and your own enterprises to invest in their life. That's where it starts. Paul's love for the churches in the areas that he evangelized repeatedly comes out in his letters to those churches. For example, in Philippians 1:8, Paul says to the Philippian church, *". . . how greatly I long after you all . . . ."* In 1 Thessalonians 3:10 he says, *"Night and day praying exceedingly that we might see your face, and might perfect that which is lacking in your faith."* And in 2 Corinthians 12:15 he says, *"And I will very gladly spend and be spent for you; though the more abundantly I love you, the less I be loved."* He gave himself to those people, didn't he?

Love is the key to follow-up. Don't hand someone eight books of follow-up. Give him your life and your heart. Another thing we're to do in follow-up is to . . .

B. **Warn (Admonish) Them** (v. 14c)

   ". . . I warn you."

   You can't raise a child by doing nothing more than just affirming your love. You also have to warn them, don't you? You have to say, "If you keep doing that, you're going to have a problem." That's what the Bible calls *admonishing*. Admonishing is defined as "warning with a view toward judgment." So, if you really want to follow somebody up, you have to warn them about the way they are going. Warning is a key element.

   Another element of follow-up is that we need to . . .

C. **Be an Example to Them** (v. 17a)

   "For this cause have I sent unto you Timothy, who is my beloved son and faithful in the Lord, who shall bring you into remembrance of my ways which are in Christ . . ."

In other words, Paul says, "I'm going to send a guy to you who's just like me. You can follow him." In 1 Corinthians 11:1, Paul said, *"Be ye followers of me, even as I also am of Christ."* I think it's critical to be an example. You say, "How am I going to be an example?" Just get your life alongside their life, and just keep walking your Christian walk so that they can see how it's done. That is one of the most powerful elements of follow-up there is. Why? Because you're one on one, teaching them biblical living and a sanctified life-style.

A fourth element of follow-up is that we must . . .

D. Teach Them (v. 17b)

". . . as I teach everywhere in every church."

I think follow-up involves input—telling them the truth of God they need to hear.

Finally, follow-up requires that we . . .

E. Discipline Them (vv. 18-21)

In verses 18-21, Paul goes on to talk about the fact that if the Corinthians don't shape up, he's going to come with a rod. That's referring to discipline. There are times when we have to discipline folks. How do you discipline somebody you're following up? Confront them verbally, and say, "Hey, you've got to stop doing that. Let me help you change that pattern in your life." There has to be a willingness to confront. You say, "I don't want to say anything about their problems. Who am I to do that? I have problems in my own life." Well, get the beam out of your own eye and then work on the one in their eye. But you can't leave them alone. You're not going to help them if you don't say what ought to be said.

Well, I hope those things give you a basic start. We've talked about who can witness, and we've said that anybody who's a Christian can witness, must witness, and does witness. Why? Because they've had a personal relationship with Jesus Christ. We've also said that witnessing is simply giving testimony to the watching world that Jesus Christ is who He says He is, and that He can do what He says He can do. We've talked about the fact that witnessing is essential and that there's a sacrificial price to pay. We've said it's necessary because we're commanded to do it and equipped to do it. And then we've talked about some of the features that make witnessing effective. We've talked about methods—how to use our personal testimony and the Word of God—and we've talked about follow-up. That's all of it in one little package. So, if we can work on these things and internalize them a little at a time, and put them into practice as we communicate Christ, I believe God will be honored in the way that we witness.

Focusing on the Facts

1. According to John 15:26-27, what is one of the ministries of the Holy Spirit? How does He accomplish this ministry? (see p. 67)
2. How does the Apostle John define a witness? (see p. 68)
3. What is the prerequisite for being a witness for Jesus Christ? (see pp. 68-69)
4. Is witnessing only for pastors and people with the gift of evangelism? Support your answer with Scripture. (see p. 69)
5. Can a Christian be a witness without ever opening his mouth? Explain. (see p. 69)
6. What will people conclude if they know that you are a Christian, but you never talk to them about Christ? (see p. 69)
7. Explain the following statement: The issue isn't whether or not you are a witness, the issue is what kind of witness you are. (see pp. 69-70)
8. What is the technical definition of witnessing? (see p. 70)
9. In the analogy of Christ being on trial in a court of law, who is the jury? Who is the defense lawyer? Who are the witnesses? Who is the prosecutor? Where is the courtroom? (see p. 70)
10. How does the element of sacrifice relate to witnessing? (see p. 71)
11. What are some of the effects that will occur when the gospel is truly proclaimed? (see p. 71)
12. Should witnessing consist of more than a discussion of God's love and the benefits of the Christian life? If so, what else needs to be communicated? Why? (see p. 72)
13. What character trait do we see lived out in the story of John Paton on pages 72-73?
14. If God sovereignly brings men to Himself in salvation, why are we to witness? Should the understanding of why we're to witness have any relationship to whether or not we do it? (see p. 74)
15. What was Charles Spurgeon's reply to the question of why he didn't preach only to the elect? What was the point of his reply? (see p. 74)
16. Will God send someone to hell who has never heard the gospel? Explain. (see p. 74)
17. Must we be specially trained to witness? Explain. (see p. 75)
18. Why are the personal testimonies that are given in a baptismal service so effective in showing the power of God? What does this say about a requirement to be formally trained to witness? (see p. 75)
19. What are the four overall elements of effective witnessing? (see pp. 76-80)

20. Explain why the corporate testimony of a pure church is foundational to witnessing. (see p. 76)

21. In what way is our effectiveness in witnessing dependent upon other Christians? (see p. 77)

22. Why does Paul tell Timothy and Titus to choose leaders in the church who are blameless and above reproach? (see p. 77)

23. From a human perspective, why is it oftentimes hardest to win members of your own family to Christ? (see p. 78)

24. Are the corporate testimony of a pure church and the individual testimony of a pure life enough to bring someone to a saving knowledge of Christ? What else must occur? (see p. 78)

25. Receptivity to the gospel often starts with a _____ _____. (see p. 78)

26. What important principles of evangelism are taught in the parable of the rich young ruler in Matthew 19:16-22? (see pp. 78-80)

27. When you're witnessing, why is it so important to recognize your dependency on the power of the Holy Spirit? (see p. 80)

28. What are the specific ways that the Holy Spirit is involved in the salvation process? (see pp. 80-81)

29. What are the six elements involved in the method of effective witnessing? (see pp. 81-83)

30. Is it important to share your personal testimony when you're witnessing to someone? Why? (see p. 81)

31. When you're explaining your conversion to someone, why should you incorporate Scripture? (see p. 82)

32. In order for someone to come to Christ, must he understand the full implications of repentance and the Lordship of Christ? Explain. (see p. 83)

33. Read 1 Corinthians 4:14-21. What are the five responsibilities that we have in following up a new Christian? (see pp. 83-85)

34. What is the key to follow-up? What does this mean? How is this accomplished? (see pp. 83-84)

Pondering the Principles
(For Group Discussion)

1. Is the knowledge of a specific method of evangelism an absolute necessity in order to witness? What is required for a person to be an effective witness? Do methods of evangelism have their place? If so, what is that place?

2. What do you say to someone who tells you that Christians should keep their religion to themselves instead of proselytizing from other religions, because everyone should be able to worship God in their own way?

3. When people know that you claim to be a Christian, does it affect the way you act around them? Should it? Why or why not? What statement are you making to people who know that you're a Christian, if you never talk to them about Christ?

4. Should we expect to get reactions from people when we witness? Why? What could be wrong if you're not getting reactions?

5. Can you think of a time when the fear of being ridiculed prevented you from witnessing? Describe that situation. What personal perspective would give you victory over that fear? What steps can you take to develop that perspective in your life?

6. Why isn't it necessary for us to understand how our witnessing relates to God's sovereign call in salvation? Perhaps the strongest reason that we're to witness is the fact that we're commanded to. In essence, what are we saying to God when we don't do something He's commanded, simply because we don't understand the reasons behind His command?

7. As you witness, the following question will inevitably come up: "If Christianity is the only way to heaven, what about all the people in the world who have never heard of Jesus Christ? Will they go to hell if they haven't accepted Christ as their Lord and Savior?" What's your answer to that objection? Read the following verses: Psalm 19:1-2; Romans 1:18-21; John 14:6; Acts 4:12. How do these verses apply to this issue?

8. How does your personal purity affect the credibility of your church's corporate witness in the community? How does this relate to the practice of church discipline?

9. Using Matthew 19:16-22, discuss how self-esteem can serve as a barrier in receiving Christ as Lord and Savior.

10. How can we sometimes con people into becoming Christians? Why does this happen? What are some practical steps to avoid doing this?

11. What are the six elements involved in the method of effective witnessing? Discuss the importance of each step and the reason behind it.

12. Of the five responsibilities of follow-up seen in 1 Corinthians 4:14-21, which are you the strongest in? Which are you the weakest in? What steps can you take to strengthen those weak areas?

DISCUSSION GUIDE

	Focusing on the Facts	*Pondering the Principles*
How to Study the Bible		
Question #1	1-2	1-2
Question #2	3-16	3-5
Question #3	17-18	6
Question #4	19-23	7
Question #5	24-29	8-9
How to Pray		
Question #1	1-8	1-3
Question #2	9	4
Question #3	10-21	5-8
Question #4	22-27	9-11
Question #5	28	12
How to Fellowship		
Question #1	1-5	1-2
Question #2	6-9	3-4
Question #3	10-14	5
Question #4	15-25	6-7
Question #5	26-40	8-10
How to Witness		
Question #1	1-7	1-3
Question #2	8-13	4-5
Question #3	14-18	6-7
Question #4	19-32	8-11
Question #5	33-34	12